MELISSA MAY

Grace Norris Salisbury

World rights reserved. This book or any portion thereof may not be copied or reproduced in any form or manner whatever, except as provided by law, without the written permission of the publisher, except by a reviewer who may quote brief passages in a review.

The author assumes full responsibility for the accuracy of all facts and quotations as cited in this book. The opinions expressed in this book are the author's personal views and interpretations, and do not necessarily reflect those of the publisher.

This book is provided with the understanding that the publisher is not engaged in giving spiritual, legal, medical, or other professional advice. If authoritative advice is needed, the reader should seek the counsel of a competent professional.

Copyright © 2025 Grace Norris Salisbury
Copyright © 2025 TEACH Services, Inc.
Published in Calhoun, Georgia, USA
ISBN-13: 978-1-4796-1800-2 (Paperback)
ISBN-13: 978-1-4796-1801-9 (ePub)
Library of Congress Control Number: 2024923906

All Scripture quotations are taken from the King James Version. Public domain.

Table of Contents

Introduction		5
Chapter 1	The Beginning	7
Chapter 2	Good Times and Bad Times	16
Chapter 3	Sad Farewell	25
Chapter 4	A Home of Her Own	33
Chapter 5	New Adventures	42
Chapter 6	Better Times	51
Chapter 7	Alden's Disguise	59
Chapter 8	Plains Valley	68
Chapter 9	Jack and the Longhorns	77
Chapter 10	Another Move	85
Chapter 11	Suwano's Enterprise—Selby's Story	94
Chapter 12	Lydia's Independence	103
Chapter 13	Another Milestone	113
Chapter 14	A Fight	121
Chapter 15	Returning Home	130
Chapter 16	Accepting Truth	139
Conclusion		150

Introduction

One bright summer morning when I was a teenager, living with my parents on a small hillside farm in western Oregon, I glanced out the kitchen window and saw a familiar figure coming down the old mountain road which joined the main road just below our place. It was Grandma.

Until then I had no enthusiasm for my chore of washing the breakfast dishes, but seeing that Grandma was coming, I hurried to finish my morning tasks, for I did not want to miss any of the conversation while she was visiting in our home. And I wondered, as I hastened to put the kitchen in order, if ever anyone else had a grandmother like ours.

Others may have been just as dear to the hearts of their children, grandchildren, and great grandchildren as Grandma was to us, but in our circle of relatives and friends, there was no one else like her. The stories she told were favorites with youngsters of all ages in our family, just as she herself was a favorite with old and young alike. And those stories were all true experiences from her own life and that of her family. I often thought that those stories should all be written out so others might enjoy them too, and that I would like to do the writing.

The special photo taken in honor of Grandma Melissa May's ninetieth birthday.

It must have been twenty years later when I looked out another kitchen window, from another home on another hillside, and saw Grandma coming to visit us once more. Although there were other visits before, after, and in between these two, in my memory these are outstanding. We were planning to celebrate her ninetieth birthday in a few days, and she was on her way up our steep hillside from the canyon below because she wanted me to take a picture of her with my two daughters in honor of the occasion. And still those stories had not been written.

Grandma was no longer with us when I finally began collecting the story material, and then I found that each story represented a bit of her life and so could not stand alone but needed to be woven together with the shining threads of her character and personality to give them life and meaning.

The story of Melissa May has been built out of the many incidents and short stories told by my grandmother as remembered and retold by her four daughters. Some folks keep a diary in a book, but Grandma wrote hers in the hearts of her children.

Once part of the first frontier west of the Allegheny Mountains, northwestern Pennsylvania was a picturesque country of hills, valleys, and streams, settled by farmers, when Melissa was born on June 11, 1854. Her family lived near Oil City, in Venango County where oil was often seen on the water of the small streams, but at that time little use had been found for this oil which would later become a great industry.

Melissa's arrival brought the family count up to seven: mother, father, and five children. Kate was nearly two years old, Selby was next older, then Jennie, and the oldest child was Melinda. Their mother had been Martha Wilson before her marriage to Jackson Barnes, who was a carpenter by trade and also a shoemaker.

Chapter 1

The Beginning

It was late afternoon, and the chilly air was hinting of snow soon to fall, as Jackson Barnes stepped out of the general store. He turned up the collar of his coat against the cold and started walking toward home, but his thoughts lingered on the subject which had been under discussion in the store before he left.

A few lazy snowflakes began falling as he walked along, and soon there were many coming down, but he scarcely noticed them until he neared his own home and heard the voices of his children as they came out to enjoy the sight of the first snowfall of the season.

"I like to watch the snowflakes coming down, don't you?" Jennie asked, not expecting an answer. "There comes a big one," she added, reaching out as if to catch it; then she was off on a merry chase, for the snowflake veered away from her outstretched hand.

Melinda stayed on the porch, watching her sister and brother from that protected area.

"Tomorrow we can have more fun out in the snow," she remarked cheerfully. "Now there isn't even enough to make a snowball. Come on, let's go back inside. It's cold out here, and you know Ma said we shouldn't stay out very long."

But Selby did not hear her for he had run ahead of the girls and down the path toward the gate. Then, seeing that their father was coming along the road, he paused to look back and make the announcement.

"Pa's coming," he shouted, and then started out to meet him.

"Let's wait till they get here before we go back in the house," Jennie suggested, as both girls stood looking in the direction of the road.

Inside the house their little sister Kate had been watching at the window, and she, too, saw her father coming.

"Papa," she announced.

"Is your pa coming?" Martha asked from the next room. Then she came in, carrying the baby in her arms, to stand beside her daughter at the window.

"Papa?" the little girl repeated, this time a question.

"Yes, Kate, that is Papa coming all right," her mother answered as she turned to put the baby in the cradle before going into the kitchen to start preparation of the evening meal.

"Everything will be covered with snow when we wake up in the morning, won't it, Pa?" Jennie asked as she and the other two children followed their father toward the door.

"It certainly will," he answered. "But now we must go inside, for you are not dressed warmly enough to be out in the cold, and it must be about supper time."

That evening, after the children were all settled in bed for the night, Martha got out her basket of mending and came to sit by the fire with her husband. She knew that he had something on his mind, and she thought she knew just what it was.

"Did you hear any news when you were in town this afternoon?" she asked.

"Not much of anything new, I guess, Martha," he answered. "Silas Baker had a newspaper from the city again, but most of the talk at the store was about going west. You know, of course, that Si is planning to go west in the spring."

"Yes, I know," she agreed. "Ever since my brother went out to Iowa, it seems that more and more folks have been moving out there or making plans to go. With most of my family already out there now, I have been wondering if we, too, might be able to go this next spring."

She paused, thinking not only of her own parents, and younger brothers and sisters who had gone the year before, but also of the many fascinating tales which were being circulated about that country. Men who had returned from the "West" spread stories about it, and there were stories in the newspapers. She knew many people who were talking about moving west. The fame of Iowa's rich soil, which was selling for only a dollar and twenty-five cents an acre, was a big attraction. A great migration was in progress.

"I think perhaps we can be ready to go then," her husband finally answered, interrupting her thoughts. "Iowa sounds like a pretty good place; it may be the land of opportunity for us as well as many others."

"It would be good to see my folks again, and I know the children will all be excited about it," Martha commented. "But we will need to plan carefully so we will be ready to leave as early as possible; with the first group to go if we can."

The restless, migratory spirit of the people in our country during this period of our history was the true pioneer spirit. Men hoped to make better homes for their families in the West where a bright future seemed to await them just for the taking. It certainly did seem that Iowa was a land of opportunity for those who were adventuresome enough to attempt making a new start in a new land.

The Barnes family would not be moving as many things as some did, for they were not rich in this world's goods, and Martha had none of the conveniences of our day in her home. Some of the early inventions of our machine age had already been introduced at that time, but they would seem quite primitive to us now. There were washing machines, and more recently the sewing machine had come into use, but no doubt there were people on the ever-moving frontier who had never seen either one of these machines.

"It looks like we need a log for the fire," Martha remarked one evening, as she began clearing the table after their evening meal.

"I'll go bring one in," her husband told her as he rose from his chair at the table. He raked up the coals in the fireplace, ready for the new log, and went outside to get it.

As her father went out, Melinda came into the room, carrying the baby. She had been instructed to take care of Melissa while her mother was busy in the kitchen.

"Let's walk," she said companionably to the little girl as she put her down and took her by the hand. Melinda liked to give her little sister lessons in learning, for she had just begun to walk a few steps at a time by herself. Leading the baby over to one side of the fireplace where she could balance herself, unaided, by leaning against the wall, Melinda left her there.

Melissa started walking unsteadily across the smooth hearth toward her sister's outstretched arms, but she was unable to complete the journey. Losing her balance, she started falling toward the open fire so close beside her.

"Here's a nice smooth place for you to walk," she said, as she began backing away until she was across the hearth from the baby.

"Come on, Lizzie, she coaxed, as she held out her arms invitingly toward the hesitating child. "Come and walk over here to me."

Melissa started walking unsteadily across the smooth hearth toward her sister's outstretched arms, but she was unable to complete the journey. Losing her balance, she started falling toward the open fire so close beside her.

Melinda's frightened outcry, as she started toward the kitchen to get her mother, brought Martha rushing to the scene. Melissa's wail of pain brought an abrupt end to both work and play for the family, as her hands came in contact with the hot coals, but this saved the baby face, and Martha quickly rescued her so that only the little hands were badly burned.

Father Barnes went at once to get a doctor, who was able to treat the burns so that the pain somewhat eased, but it was a long time before she would use her hands for anything. For a while her parents feared that Melissa might lose the use of her hands altogether, so they were much relieved when she started doing things with her hands once again. But the scars from this experience ever remained on her hands.

Sometime after the little scarred hands were well again, Martha was busy with household tasks one afternoon when suddenly the door opened. Looking up from her work, she was surprised to see her husband standing in the entrance. He did not usually come home in mid-afternoon, so she guessed that he had something of importance to discuss with her and waited for him to speak.

"The Bakers and several families have decided to leave for Iowa just as soon as they can," he announced, "so if we are to go with them, we should begin getting things ready to go."

"I will be glad to be near my folks again, but Jackson, are you sure this is what you want to do? None of your family is out there."

"I'm sure this will be the best thing for us to do," he replied, "and perhaps some of my folks will be going later. Bill has talked some about it. Now, I think that we have already gotten most of the things we will need after we get there, as much as we can afford anyway, but we had better start planning now for what we will need along the way. We should be ready to go by the first of the month if we expect to get there and get settled before cold weather comes."

"All right then, it's settled," was Martha's only comment.

Preparations were soon begun in earnest for the long trip to Iowa. Parents, children, grandparents, aunts and uncles, and friends of those who were planning to go, all took an interest in this work. Baby Melissa was about the only one not much concerned about these preparations going on in the Barnes household.

Frames were built onto their wagons, and canvas covers to fit over the frames were made, thus converting them into "Prairie Schooners." Under these covers their household goods would be protected from the weather while they traveled, and the children could ride most of the way, the younger ones especially.

Everything could not be taken along, so decisions had to be made as to what would be most needed and what must be left behind. Property was sold, and more things purchased for use on the journey. Then they loaded the wagons, said goodbye to friends, neighbors, and relatives who would remain behind, and turned their eyes westward as the wagons started rolling on the road toward Iowa.

Some people went part of the way by boats but travel by wagon was the method chosen by most of those who were going west, and the overland routes were deeply marked by the wheels of the many wagons that had gone before. At times there seemed to be oceans of wagons headed west, and it was a common sight to see a group of wagons formed into an encampment for the night along the way. Somewhere in this "sea of white-tipped ships of the prairie" were the wagons carrying Melissa and her loved ones on their way west.

At sunset the wagon trains usually stopped to make camp for the night, and the evening meal was often prepared over an open campfire. When the Barnes and Wilson families reached the city of Chicago, their little caravan camped by the lake. The children had never seen such a large body of water, so the sight of Lake Michigan was a new and interesting experience for them.

In the morning, as the campers were preparing to resume their journey, Selby discovered that his dog was missing. After going all around their camp, calling and looking without success, he came to his father, looking as if he were about to cry, for he was very fond of his pet.

"I wonder what's the matter with Selby," his mother remarked as she saw him coming.

"Pa, I can't find Rover anywhere," the little boy lamented.

"Did you call him, son?" his father asked.

"Oh yes, Pa," was the answer, "I've called and called, and looked all around everywhere for him."

"Well, we will see if we can find him," Jackson promised. "Why don't you get the girls to help you look, and we'll wait awhile before we go on."

Because the children were all anxious about the dog, the family group stayed beside the lake for several hours, hoping to locate the pet, but the little dog did not return, nor could they find any trace of him, so finally they started on without him, much to Selby's disappointment. It was thought perhaps someone had stolen the dog or that he might have been killed.

When travelers came near hostile Indian Territory, they found it would not be safe for them to travel on as a small group. They would have to wait until there were 100 wagons ready to go through. Just a short time before this a whole wagon train had been wiped out by the Indians. It had been a massacre—the people were killed, and their cattle, horses, and everything they had that the Indians wanted had been carried away. So now the government sent soldiers to escort the travelers through the hostile area if they waited until a group of 100 were ready to go at one time.

Sometimes heavy rains made travel difficult. When the wagon wheels became mired in the mud so they would not move, the wagon might have to be unloaded before it could be pulled out. Most travelers were willing to help others when they had trouble along the way.

Many streams had to be crossed, some large and some small, but in places along the larger rivers there were ferries to take the wagons and cattle over. Finally they came to the Mississippi River, where they found many others awaiting their turn to be taken across.

The great tide of covered wagons from the east flowed into the Mississippi Valley, out onto the rich prairie land, and some of it went on further west. Some groups settled together, while others scattered as each family chose their new location. Melissa and her family traveled well across the state of Iowa before they reached their new home.

Iowa, said to mean "The Beautiful Land," was described as Canaan for the children of the eastern states. It was a land of prairie, groves, and meandering streams; an open country very different from the small valleys and tree-covered hills which most of the migrants had left behind in the east. There were no mountains to make travel difficult, so it was possible to cross the state in most any direction without constructing roads or trails. But this beautiful land could become mysterious and terrifying at times because of storm, grass fires, mirages, the cold, and the loneliness.

"Well, here we are," Jackson Barnes announced one day as the wagons rolled to a stop near what appeared to be a small country store.

These were pleasant words to the ears of the weary travelers. They had arrived at Hometown, which was not far from Grandfather Wilson's new home. Later the name of this little place was changed to Lewis.

"But where is our house?" asked one of the children.

"Where's Grandpa?" asked another.

Before long they had the answers to these and many other questions. John Wilson, the children's grandfather, came and led the way to their new location. From Hometown they went west, just over into Pottawatomie County, and chose land near the Nishnabotna River. Their new home was about forty-five miles east of Council Bluffs, which was a city of less than 1,000 inhabitants at that time.

The prairie all around them was covered with tall blue stem grass about two feet high, and when the wind blew, it looked like one vast field of grain waving in the breeze.

There were other families near, that is, most of them lived a mile or more away. Some had built sod houses in which to live temporarily, but Melissa and her family lived in a frame house. Stables were sometimes built of grass, and Jackson Barnes made one of these for his livestock. Two rows of posts, or poles, were driven into the ground quite close together, and then the dry grass, or hay, was stuffed in between the rows. Thus the walls were made, and after they were finished, a roof of poles and grass was put on.

There was much to be done in preparation for the first winter, and when it came, the settlers soon learned that it could become unpleasant at times, even dangerous, to be out in a storm. Often, during a blizzard, the prairie became one vast expanse of white with all landmarks hidden by the flying snow. Then no living thing could travel safely, or stay alive without shelter of some kind. The children soon learned that snow was not always fun. The first winter was the hardest in this new land.

Early in the spring the farmers began getting the tough prairie sod ready for planting, and this was hard work where ground had never been broken before. Gashes were cut in the sod with an ax for planting corn; small grain was sown by hand.

In early summer the prairie grass was ready to cut for hay.

The older children usually had their share of work, helping indoors and out by taking care of younger children, working in the garden, and doing many chores and errands. But it all seemed worthwhile to both the children and the parents because they had hopes and plans for a better future.

A flaxen-haired baby brother joined the family circle in August of 1856. Within a year this baby brother had become Melissa's favorite playmate. His name was Robert, and the two little children spent many happy hours together in play while the older ones were attending a small school located about a mile away from home.

One winter Jackson Barnes became ill, so Mother Martha had all the work to do with what help the children could give her. That was a hard winter for most everyone on the prairie. Iowa history tells of a panic in 1857, so perhaps this was the same year.

During a high wind the prairie grass caught fire. A prairie fire can be very dangerous because it moves so rapidly in the dry grass. This caused a great deal of damage, destroying the stables and the hay they had stacked as winter feed for the stock.

In the house, on their beds, were mattresses made of ticking and stuffed with hay, and thankful that their home had escaped the flames, they gladly removed the hay from the beds and fed it to the horses to keep them from starving before other feed could be obtained for them.

Timber grew along the rivers, but there was not enough for all needs, so when they did not have coal, sometimes corncobs, twisted hay, and even ears of corn were used for fuel.

By 1859, when Melissa was five years old, things had begun to improve, and the future seemed much brighter again. Then it was that calamity struck.

Martha awoke one morning with a terrible headache.

"Perhaps you should stay in bed," her husband told her. "Selby can get a fire started for you while I go out to start the chores."

After Selby had a fire going, Martha got up to make coffee, thinking it might make her feel better to drink some. As she reached for the coffee on the shelf, she seemed to become blinded; she could not see it.

"Selby, where's the coffee? I can't see it," she said. Then she fell, unconscious, to the floor.

Selby ran out and called his father, and together they picked her up and carried her back to bed, but in spite of anything they could do, she never regained consciousness. In a short time, she was dead.

This was a real tragedy for the family of young children and their father. Bobby was only about three years old, and Melissa was five. They were still too young to understand much about what had happened, or to wonder what would happen to them in the future without a mother. They only knew that their mother was not in her usual place in the home, and they missed her very much.

According to the custom of the time, the mother's body was dressed and laid out in an adjoining room, covered with a sheet. Melissa knew that her mother was in that room and felt that she must see her.

"Come, Bobby," she said, taking her brother by the hand when she thought no one was noticing what they were doing. "Let's go find Mama."

She opened the door, and they tiptoed softly into the room where their mother lay asleep in death. There they stood, just inside the room, for a while, hand in hand, not knowing just what to do. Death is so final in this mortal life, and although they did not understand, they already felt some of the loneliness and bewilderment of motherless children. Soon they turned and hurriedly left the room, carefully closing the door behind them as they went out.

After his wife's death, Jackson Barnes soon realized that he was not able to keep the children and home together, so he began looking for homes where his children might be welcomed.

Martha's parents talked it over and decided that they could take the baby.

"We would like to keep Bobby," they told their son-in-law. "We can give him a home and keep him with us until he is old enough to make his own way." Of course they knew that Jackson Barnes might get married again someday and want his little son with him again, but until and unless that happened, they would take care of him.

"That will be fine," his father decided, after thinking it over a bit. "I'm very glad to know that he will have a good home."

Before long the four older children were placed in homes where they could work for their room and board. But what was to become of Melissa?

Well, she too, was taken to her Grandparents home, but it was only a temporary arrangement in her case, for she was to stay there only until another place could be found for her. Sad to say, the two little playmates were to be separated, but they would be together for a while, and, too young to understand the situation or to dwell on their sorrow long, they were soon happily romping about the Wilson home together.

Chapter 2

Good Times and Bad Times

The Wilson family took good care of their vegetable garden and tried to preserve it from harm, for it furnished a very important part of their food supply. Grandfather noticed that the potato bugs were beginning to eat holes in the leaves of his potato vines, so he decided it was time to take action against them before they did more damage.

"Come, children," he said one morning as Melissa and Bobby were about to leave the breakfast table to play. "We have some work to do in the garden today."

"What are we going to do?" Melissa asked.

"You just come along with me, and I will show you what we are going to do," he answered as the children started to follow him outside.

Grandfather found a tin can for each of the children and one for himself, and they went out to the potato patch. There he pointed out one of the yellow beetles with black stripes on its wings and instructed the children to look for those bugs.

Soon all three were busy picking the bugs off the vines and putting them into the cans or knocking them into the cans with sticks.

These beetles were, like the Indians, natives of this country, and before the settlers came west, they had fed upon certain wild plants. But after they found the garden potato, they really had a feast, and multiplied more rapidly, spreading eastward. They ate the leaves and vines and laid their eggs on the underside of the leaves they did not eat.

Soon those eggs would hatch into grubs, and they too started eating. So the beetles had to be destroyed or there would be few potatoes for the family's winter food supply.

As the children and their grandfather worked and talked, a man was driving his team and wagon along the road toward the farm. Bobby was the first to notice them coming.

"Who's that?" he asked.

Both children watched as the man guided his team into the lane and to their grandparent's home.

"Can't tell from here whether I know the man or not," Grandfather answered, "but I had better go and see what he wants. You children stay here and go on with your work."

The stranger started toward the house, but Grandfather called to him, so he turned and started across the yard toward the garden. It was then that Grandfather recognized him as a farmer who lived some miles distant with whom he was not personally acquainted.

"How do you do, Mr. Wilson," the man said as soon as they were close enough together for talk. "I have been told that you have a little girl here who is in need of a home."

"Why yes, we do, Mr. Smith. My little granddaughter, Melissa Barnes, needs a home. She is out in the garden now with her little brother. You may have heard that their mother died recently, and their father is not able to keep the family all together, so we are taking the little boy. These are the two youngest ones, and Lizzie is five years old."

As he spoke, Grandfather was thinking that this might be a good home for the little girl.

"My wife and I have no children of our own," the farmer said, "so when we heard about this little girl, we talked it over and decided we would like to have her come and live with us. I came to see if I could take her home with me."

Mary, youngest of the Wilson family, was summoned by her father.

"Go fetch Lizzie," he instructed. "She's out in the garden with Bobby."

Then, as the men continued their conversation, Mary went out to get the children. She found them glad for an excuse to stop working.

"Lizzie, Pa wants you up at the house."

"What does he want me for?" the little girl asked.

"You'll find out when you get there," was her aunt's only reply.

By the time the children reached the house, all arrangements had been made for Melissa to leave at once for her new home.

"Mary, go in the house and get Lizzie's things ready to go," her father said. The time of parting had arrived.

Aunt Mary soon returned, carrying Melissa's sunbonnet and a small bundle which contained the few pieces of other clothing that belonged to the girl. She put the sunbonnet on her niece's head and tied it for her. Then Melissa was all ready to go.

It was hard to say goodbye to her grandfather and grandmother, but it was hardest of all to go away from her little brother playmate. Bobby may not have understood that his sister was leaving to stay away, but Melissa knew.

She did not cry or say a word, but it seemed to her as if her heart would surely break. She followed the man out to his team and wagon, climbed into the back of the wagon, and sat down behind the seat where the farmer would sit. Soon they were off.

It was not until they drove away from the Wilson home that Melissa gave way to tears. She pulled her sunbonnet down over her face as best she could so the man would not see her crying. To be taken away from the little brother she loved so much seemed like more than she could bear. She did not know if she would ever see her grandparents and Bobby again. All she knew was that she was being taken away somewhere to live with people she did not know, and where her brother would not be, nor any of her other loved ones either.

It was sunset when they arrived at the farm, and as the wagon came to a stop near the door of the small house, the farmer's wife came out to greet them.

"Well, here we are," Mr. Smith said, "and this is Melissa Barnes."

"Hello, Melissa," the lady said, as she helped the little girl out of the wagon. "It's nice to have you come to live with us. Come inside and we will have supper right away."

Mrs. Smith was glad to have the little girl and tried to make friends with her while the farmer put his wagon and team away for the night. But to Melissa, this looked like a very lonely place because there were no other children.

Although the farmer and his wife did their best to make Melissa comfortable and content, this home proved to be a very lonesome place for Melissa, who had always been with five brothers and sisters and never away from her own family group before.

Here the little scarred hands began their service for others in exchange for a home. There were many small tasks which Melissa could do to help Mrs. Smith around the home, but there was also plenty of time in which to think about her own loved ones, especially on days when the farmer and his wife did their trading in town and left her at home alone.

On those days they left very early in the morning and were sometimes quite late in returning. It took the whole day for the drive to the town, their shopping, and the return trip. While Mr. and Mrs. Smith were away, Melissa's only companion during the long hours was a large dog.

After she finished the little tasks which had been assigned to her, and she became tired of playing alone and with the dog, the time seemed to go by more slowly. And as the hours dragged along, how she wished that she could be with her little brother so they might be spending the time playing happily together. She also thought of her mother and wished that she could be with her.

As evening drew near, the little girl and the big dog would watch together for the return of the farmer and his wife. Often it would be dark before they would hear the tramp of the horse's hooves and the rumble of the wagon wheels which told them the couple were returning. And sometimes Melissa would be fast asleep before they arrived.

Thus several months passed by, and then one day Mr. Smith came home from a trip to the post office with a letter for his wife which contained news that would make quite a change in their plans. It was a sad letter, for it told of her sister's death.

"She leaves two little girls," Mrs. Smith said to her husband through her tears, "and their father wants to know if we would take them into our home and care for them, since we have no children of our own. What do you think about that?"

"Certainly we will take them, if that is what you want to do," was his answer. "They would be almost like our own, and I think we should give them a home, don't you?"

She nodded in agreement. "But what about Lizzie? We cannot keep her too."

"No, we can't, so I will take her back to her grandparent's home as soon as I have the time to go."

Melissa was very happy with this news, but she did not feel free to act excited about it in front of the farmer and his wife.

"Oh, I'm so glad, so glad," she confided to her playmate when she was alone with the big dog. "I do so want to see Bobby and Grandma and Grandpa again! Now I'm going back, and I hope it will be real soon." But it seemed like a long time before the farmer was ready to take her back to her grandfather's home.

When that happy day finally arrived, Melissa gladly gathered up her few belongings and climbed into the wagon again, thinking how nice it would be to see her loved ones again.

For several days before they started on this trip, rain had been falling, so the river they had to cross on the way was much deeper than when they had crossed it before. Water came up into the wagon bed where Melissa was sitting, and her clothing was soon very wet. But she did not mind the water very much—she was too happy about going home to Grandfather's house to worry about getting wet.

What wonderful times the two children had together again at the home of their grandparents! No one else came to get Melissa and take her home with them.

The children slept in the attic and the stairway came down into the kitchen. At the foot of these stairs was the trapdoor entrance to the cellar under the house. Whenever anyone went down to get something from the cellar, this door had to be open.

One morning Grandmother had the cellar door open while she was down getting butter and milk for breakfast. The children were still upstairs when she went down, but they were awake and getting ready to come down.

"I'm going down now," Bobby announced, as he headed for the stairway. "Hurry up, Lizzie."

"I'm coming right behind you," she answered, as he started down the stairs. In her hurry to catch up with him, she stumbled and began to fall down the stairway. Bobby tried to catch her, but instead of helping, this only resulted in both children falling all the way down to the cellar floor below, where they landed right at Grandmother's feet.

"Oh, my! Oh, my! What will you children do next?" she exclaimed as she hastily set the butter and milk down, so she could search them for broken bones. Although they were a rather bruised pair of children, neither of them had any broken bones or other serious injuries.

"You must be more careful about coming downstairs," Grandmother warned them after the excitement of their fall had subsided. "You know, it would not be amusing if you should break an arm or a leg."

The Wilson family belonged to the United Brethren church, and they were sincerely religious people so they were strict with the children. Melissa knew that her grandmother was a good Christian woman, but she still missed her own mother very much. There seemed to be no one to take her place, so Melissa felt a need for someone to love, who would love her in return, want her, and take care of her.

A board fence enclosed the yard around the house, and like most children, Melissa and Bobby liked to play on it, climbing it like a ladder, or walking along on one of the boards while holding to a higher one, and sometimes trying to balance themselves and walk along on the topmost board unaided.

"Let's go outdoors, Lizzie. I'm tired of playing in here."

"All right," she agreed readily. "Let's go climb the fence. Maybe we can see Grandpa from out there."

Grandmother was busy indoors, but before long, her work was interrupted by Melissa's voice calling her.

"Grandma! Grandma! Come quick! Bobby's in the well!"

Running out the door and over to the unfinished well where Melissa was standing, she found that it was indeed true: Bobby was down in the well. She called for Grandfather and the boys who were working in the field, and soon after they arrived on the scene, they had the little boy rescued.

"That well should not have been left uncovered after you quit working in it," Grandmother said reproachfully to her menfolks. She also had something to say to Melissa.

"Did you push your brother off the fence so that he fell into the well?"

Melissa denied having pushed him, but Grandmother was not convinced. She still thought maybe Melissa had done it and punished her accordingly. Both children had fallen down the stairs. Perhaps if both had fallen into the well, neither would have received the blame and the punishment!

Robert was not seriously hurt from his fall, but he could have been drowned if there had been no one to see the accident and no one handy to rescue him.

Melissa did not spend all of her time playing with her little brother. There were always errands to be run, and other chores which the children could do. As the months went by, the little girl was given more work to do around the home.

When the berries ripened, Melissa was sent with Aunt Mary to pick them. They grew along the Nishnabotna River. She liked to be outdoors, and often during that spring and summer she went for walks to look at the flowers and listen to the birds.

Sometimes, while walking alone, Melissa would look up into the sky and think of her mother, believing she was up there somewhere, and wishing that she might see her and talk with her once again.

While constructing a building for someone, Jackson Barnes fell and injured his back, and after this his health began failing rapidly. His doctor said that he had consumption and advised him to leave the Iowa prairie and go to the mountains. It was thought that the consumption had developed as a result of the accident. Since this seemed to be the only hope of regaining his health, Father Barnes left for Colorado, leaving his children scattered about in their various new homes.

About this time Aunt Sarah began noticing that Melissa was able to be quite helpful. Sarah Wilson had married a man named Levi Smith, and the couple had a baby boy named Jimmy. "Ma, I think I'd like to have Lizzie come and live with us," she said to her mother when she was visiting her one day. "Don't you think she could help take care of Jimmy?"

"Yes, I suppose so. I'll see what your pa thinks of the idea."

Soon afterward Melissa found that she had to leave her brother again. Although she was going to be working for her room and board, this time it should have been more pleasant than going to work for strangers. But the baby was strong and lively, and Melissa was small for her age, so it was just about all she could do to handle him. Then, too, as it turned out, Aunt Sarah was not very kind to her young niece. She was inclined to punish a great deal, and used a whip on the girl quite often when she did not do exactly as she wished her to.

Melissa did try to please Aunt Sarah, but somehow it seemed awfully hard to do.

"Lizzie, you sit here and rock Jimmy," her aunt said on one occasion, indicating the chair where Melissa was to sit before placing the baby on her lap. "And mind that you don't let him fall." Then Aunt Sarah went on with her work, and Melissa was responsible for the baby.

As she sat holding the squirming baby, he suddenly jumped free from her grasp and fell onto the floor, headfirst. Of course, his cries brought his mother onto the scene, and Melissa received a whipping for being so careless as to drop the baby. But little Jimmy loved his cousin, and he would cry, too, when she was being punished.

"The next time you have to be punished," Aunt Sarah finally warned the girl after punishing her for some offense, "I'm going to send you out to your Uncle Levi and let him take care of you."

Melissa really did not know what that would mean, but it sounded as if Uncle Levi might be even more severe with his punishment of her than Aunt Sarah had been. The next morning, she did something which displeased her aunt again, so she was sent out where her uncle was cutting wood. Plenty of punishment material was at hand here, so he picked up a suitable switch, and was about to use it, when he noticed something which caused him to hesitate.

"What's this?" he asked in a surprised tone. Then he called to his wife. "Sarah! Whatever is the matter with this child's back?" Sarah did not need to answer, for it was evident to Levi what was wrong. Melissa's back was covered with the marks of Aunt Sarah's whippings. Needless to say, she did not receive a whipping that morning, and she found that Uncle Levi was not such a dire threat after all.

Now that the brothers and sisters were all in different homes, they did not often see each other. Bobby continued to have a home with his grandparents. Jennie was with some people who ran a hotel, working for them. Selby was working for his keep for a farmer.

In 1862 the father-in-law of this farmer took Selby with him to help drive sixty head of cattle across the plains to Colorado. Selby had to walk most of the way, as there was only one horse to ride. This trip was an interesting experience for the eleven-year-old boy, but what was even more exciting, his father found him after they got to their destination.

Jackson Barnes had settled on Clear Creek, north of Denver, and although the man had not heard anything from his children since he left Iowa, and did not know Selby had come to Colorado, he happened to visit the locality where Selby was to see a man whom he had known "back in the States." There he learned of his son's whereabouts, so father and son were accidentally reunited.

Father Barnes had a small quartz mill about sixty miles from where he found his son, in the Rocky Mountains, so he took Selby there when he went back.

Meanwhile, back in Iowa, Aunt Sarah had found a place for Melissa to stay and help take care of another baby. Mrs. Hawes said the girl could go to school part of the time while staying with her, and this was pleasing news to Melissa, for she liked school and was anxious to attend.

But after she went to live with Mrs. Hawes, she soon found that she could not go to school very much. That lady decided she could not spare Melissa from her work, and she was allowed to attend only for a few days. This was very disappointing for Melissa.

Some of the time she didn't even have a bed to sleep on, only a pile of rags and clothing in one corner of a room for her bed. This might have been due, in part, to the fact that Melissa often had spells of nosebleeds in the night. She would be very tired, and slept soundly, not waking in the night, but when she awoke in the morning, she might find her hair matted and her pillow soaked through.

Early the next year, Father Barnes and Selby returned to Iowa. They went with an overland freight outfit as far as the Missouri River, and finding the river still frozen over, they crossed it by walking on the ice, then took a stage from there to Hometown.

Melissa was still too young to understand much about the issues involved in the war between the states, but of course, she heard talk about it, and she knew one of her uncles was in it.

Adjoining her father's farm was one owned by a widow, Mrs. Place, whose husband had been killed earlier in the war.

"Jackson, why don't you marry Bina Place?" someone had asked.

"I wouldn't marry Bina Place if she was the last woman left on the face of the earth," had been his reply.

Whether he was joking or serious about this at the time, those words had a note of finality about them. However, a few months after he came back from Colorado, Jackson Barnes married, and it was the Widow Place who became his wife.

Surprising as it was, the marriage made it possible for him to have his children with him again. Selby had continued to stay with his father. The others soon received word that they were to return home.

To Melissa, working in the Hawes home, it was especially good news. Mr. Hawes took her back to Aunt Sarah's home, and from there she walked the two miles to her grandparent's home. Her father came there to get her and Robert.

Melinda and Jennie returned home only for a short visit and then they went back to earning their own way, working in the homes of others. They were doing all right for themselves in this way and did not need to stay at home; besides, the new stepmother had children of her own and family finances were limited.

Chapter 3

A Sad Farewell

Melissa was pleased to find that one of the stepsisters was just about her own age. The two girls got along well together and became good friends. Her name was Rilla. The older one, Minerva, was not very kind, and sometimes she liked to play mean tricks on the younger children.

During the summer, when the berries were ripe, the girls were sent out berry picking together. It was tiresome work, of course, and Minerva was probably the least interested of the three in doing anything like work.

"Shhh," she whispered suddenly in the middle of an afternoon's work. "I heard something, didn't you?"

"I don't hear anything," her sister answered.

"Neither do I," Melissa agreed.

"But I heard something over there behind those bushes," Minerva insisted. This made the others fearful, but they looked and listened, and were not so sure about it.

"There, I heard it again. It's a bear!" she exclaimed in excitement, as if she had just gotten a glimpse of the animal she was imagining. "Come on, run!" And she grabbed each of them by one hand as she spoke, to pull them along with her toward home. "Let's get away from here."

So the three of them ran as fast as they could go toward home and ran all the way. Melissa felt like she was "just about run to death"; by the time they reached the house, she was so tired.

"Rilla, do you think Minerva saw anything in those bushes?" she asked, after they had rested.

"No, I don't think she heard anything," was Rilla's reply. "She was just playing one of her tricks on us so she would get out of picking any more berries this afternoon, that's what I think."

Selby was soon on good terms with his stepbrother, Tom, and the two boys enjoyed doing things together. One day while their parents were gone to town, they decided to go fishing, but they returned before their parents came back.

"Say, I'm hungry," Selby remarked as they came into the house.

"So am I," said Tom. "Let's see if we can find something to eat."

"I saw some dried apples around here somewhere once, Tom. Do you know where they are? I'd like some of those."

"So would I," Tom agreed. "And I know just where Ma put them too. They're in a box under the bed."

Off he went to the bedroom, Selby following. They located the box, pulled it out into the middle of the room, found the apples, and began to eat, knowing full well they were tasting of forbidden fruit.

The two boys were so busy eating and talking that they did not hear the approach of their parents until it was too late to put the box away and make their escape. Suddenly they realized they had to get out, or get caught, so they ran out of the room and out of the house as quickly and as quietly as they could. No one saw them leave. The other children were playing outside on the other side of the house. There sat the box of apples, opened up and in the middle of the room just awaiting discovery, which was not long in coming. With the older boys nowhere in sight, of course, they were not blamed for the misdeed.

"Lizzie! Bobby!" Bina was soon calling from the door. Knowing nothing about what awaited them, they answered and came to find out what was wanted of them.

"You children have been into my dried apples, haven't you?" she asked.

"No, we haven't," they answered together. But she was not convinced.

"Then show me your tongues," she demanded. They did this, but it did not help their cause any. "I can tell by looking at your tongues; you've been eating the apples," was the verdict, and she gave them the whipping which was due Selby and Tom.

Melissa and Bobby did not know who had been into the box of apples, but they had a pretty good idea who had done it. Afterward, when they would no longer be punished for their misdemeanor, the older boys admitted they were the guilty ones, and enjoyed telling how they avoided the punishment which they deserved. They thought it was very funny.

Tom was a lazy fellow, Melissa decided, and her opinion of him was confirmed when his mother told him to get a pail of water for her one day. Instead of going to get the water himself, Tom came looking for Melissa, and told her to get it. But Melissa's father happened to be nearby, and he overheard Tom ordering her to do his errand for him.

"Young man, you take that pail and get that water right now!" he told the boy. "The very idea of a big fellow like you trying to get a little girl to do it for you!" So Tom had to get the water himself after all.

Although Father Barnes' health seemed much improved after his return from Colorado, it was not to be a lasting improvement. Only a few months after he remarried, his health began to fail again, and he became more seriously ill than before.

Realizing that he must do what he could about getting his children placed in other homes where they would be taken care of, he called Selby to his bedside.

"Son, you better see if you can get work somewhere. Perhaps some farmer could use a boy to help with the chores and other farmwork and would give you room and board and money for clothes."

So Selby hired himself out to a farmer for eight dollars a month.

Kate was already settled with a family who wanted to keep her as their own daughter, and the two youngest were taken to their grandparents' home once again.

One day Bina fixed a bed for her husband in the back of the wagon and thus took him to the Wilson home so he could visit with Melissa and Bobby. This was the last time they saw their father.

Melissa was ten years old when her father died, and as on the two previous occasions, no permanent arrangements had been made for her, so she probably was more conscious of her orphaned state than the others.

Grandma Wilson was a careful housekeeper. During the summer months, she also kept her yard in neat order—the bare ground well swept and the flowers growing in neat, straight rows at one side near the fence. Melissa thought the flowers were very nice, and she thought of picking some of them when she walked by on her way to school, but she remembered her grandmother's warning words.

"Don't pick the flowers," she had said. For Grandma wanted them to be seen and enjoyed as they were, not picked and carried away.

Melissa thought of how nice it would be to take some of those flowers to her teacher, and one morning as she was starting on her way to school, she found a way to have some of them to give. She noticed that some of the plants nearest the fence had grown through and were blooming on the other side—outside the yard. She knew it would be wrong to pick the others, but she thought it would surely be all right to pick those that were blooming outside the fence, so she took them to her teacher.

The vegetable garden also held a special attraction for Melissa. She liked cucumbers, and it seemed that she was never allowed to eat as many of them as she wanted. This gave her an unsatisfied feeling, a craving to just eat all she wanted of them sometime.

An opportunity came for her to satisfy this longing. Her grandparents were away, and only the two children were at home, so she took this chance.

She went to the garden and picked some cucumbers, then secured a knife from the kitchen and sat down on the porch steps to eat all she wanted of them at one sitting. Bobby was warned not to tell on her, and perhaps he didn't tell.

But Melissa told on herself, because she had eaten too many of them, and she got sick—the price of overindulgence.

Her grandmother endeavored to do right according to her knowledge and belief in the Bible, and because of her faith in the Holy Scriptures as the Word of the living God, she was able to help Melissa establish a firm foundation in spiritual things. The girl felt certain that her grandmother was a good Christian woman.

But sometimes it was hard to be sure when to speak and when to be silent. Melissa did not tell anyone about it when she ran a pitchfork through her foot, fearing that she might be punished for her carelessness if it became known what she had done.

It happened when she was at the barn where she was watching her grandfather working. He had been pitching hay down for the stock from the haymow above, and when he came down, he noticed her standing nearby, so he handed the fork to her.

"Here, Lizzie, hold the pitchfork for me, will you?" he asked. "I'll want to use it again as soon as I get back."

She took it, and he went on. As she stood there idly holding the fork up by the handle, with the tines on the ground, she began jabbing the sharp tines in and out of the earth, raising the fork up to better force it into the ground each time.

One miss was enough—once missing the ground and running one of the tines through her bare foot instead. No one was near enough to see what she had done or to hear her muffled outcry, so she pulled it out and did not tell her grandfather about it when he returned.

Melissa had a sore foot for a while, and it kept her home from school, too, but her grandmother just thought it had been bruised from stepping on a sharp stone.

Sometimes people traveling through the country would stop at the Wilson home to spend a night, so when a young man of about twenty, riding a white horse, stopped there one evening, it was not thought of as an unusual event. Grandfather went to the door in answer to the knock and invited the fellow in.

He introduced himself as Alden Pettegrew, and asked if he might stay for the night, since it was getting a little late for traveling.

Grandfather agreed to put the young man up for the night, seeing that he seemed like an honest fellow in need of a night's lodging. The next morning when Alden was ready to resume his journey, he asked what the charge was, paid for it without comment, and went on his way.

"Remarkable young feller," was Grandfather's observation. "He did not make any excuses or try to get out of paying by telling me he didn't have the right change like most of them do."

Melissa was to remember this young man who came riding on a white horse, for she met him again later, under different circumstances, and came to know him very well.

Robert liked to ride the horses on his grandfather's farm. They were gentle horses, but when there was no work for them and they were kept in the barn, they had little or no exercise. Then they had to be taken out for water, and one day Robert decided to ride one of them on the way back to the barn after taking them out for a drink. He tied the team together and then mounted one. They started up so quickly, and were so frolicsome, that they were soon out of his control, and he fell off.

Melissa and her grandmother were the only ones at home when this happened. They hurried out to where he had fallen and found that he had broken his leg. It was a bad break too; the broken bone had cut through the flesh and into the ground. They carried him to the house, and a doctor was summoned to set the broken bones.

After the leg healed, they found that it had not been set very good, however, for his leg was not quite as straight as it should have been.

About a year after her father's death, Melissa was put out to work for her room and board in a home in Council Bluffs. Mrs. Grant needed a girl to help with housework and the care of her two small boys, and Melissa was pleased with the job because the Grant family lived near where her sister, Jennie, worked. When she took the little boys out for a walk, she would stop by to visit with her sister.

However, this pleasant arrangement was brought to an end when Mrs. Grant found out that Jennie was working for a saloonkeeper's family. She told Melissa she must not take her little boys there anymore. Melissa also worked awhile in the home of Mrs. Grant's sister.

While working for another family in the city, it was her chore to get the milk in the early mornings. If she did not return with the milk within the time allotted for the trip, she would get a whipping.

It was while making these early morning trips that Melissa got to thinking about how nice it would be if she could have a home with some rich folks like her sister Kate had. On the way she passed a home which she thought must belong to rich people and the idea of asking them if they would take her to live with them occurred to her. Perhaps if she would hurry on her way to get the milk the next morning, she would have time to stop there and ask.

In the morning, she ran all the way to get the milk so she would have time on her way back to stop at that place. Her knock brought a lady to the door.

"Wouldn't you like to have me come live with you and be your daughter?" she asked hopefully.

"No, I don't think we would," came the curt and disappointing reply. Then Melissa had to hurry on with the milk so she would not receive another whipping.

Seldom was she allowed to attend school regularly, for her work was of more importance to most folks than letting her have a chance to get more education from books. Melissa wanted very much to attend school and should have been given more opportunity to do so.

When Jennie found that her sister was not being allowed to go to school, she went to see the people where Melissa was working at the time and had an argument with the lady of the house about it.

Then she took her sister away from there and kept her at the hotel where she was working until another home was found where Melissa could stay and would be allowed to attend school.

Melissa was in school the day after the Council Bluffs bank was robbed. She had a girlfriend in the school whom she liked really well, but she knew that people were curious about this girl's father. The family lived at the edge of town, not far from the railroad tracks. A thicket of trees was between the house and the tracks.

This family seemed to dress and live very well, yet the father, Mr. Rogers, did not work, as far as anyone knew, though he was quite a popular fellow. At times he would be away from home for a while, however, and folks wondered why. They wondered what he did for a living.

Mr. Rogers sauntered downtown as usual that morning, but he did not linger there long after he overheard someone talking.

"I saw a handcar come down the railroad track," one fellow said to another. "It stopped near the brush by the Rogers place, and the three men who were on it all got off there."

That was when Mr. Rogers started for home. And as he hurried along, he began to realize that there were some other men heading toward his home also. Then he began to run.

The sound of running footsteps going by the schoolhouse brought the children to their feet to look out the windows. They all saw Mr. Rogers running, and they also saw the group of men who were hurrying in the same direction.

Melissa's little friend, Martha Rogers, began to cry, and asked to be excused that she might go home.

Later on Melissa heard more about what happened. The men arrived at the Rogers' house in time to catch Mr. Rogers putting money into the fire as fast as he could. When the officers of the law searched the house, they found money hidden in the mattresses, some hidden in the well curb outside the house and in other places. It was said that Mrs. Rogers had some of it hidden inside her corset.

The other two men who had been seen getting off the handcar with Mr. Rogers were also found. They were hiding in the cellar. All three were taken off to jail.

But they all broke out and escaped and were not caught again. Sometime after the escape, Mrs. Rogers and the children left the town—perhaps to join Mr. Rogers somewhere else.

Melinda also worked in Council Bluffs. Indians were quite a common sight in the town and often came to the homes of the white folks, usually to beg for something. Melinda was out on the porch of the home where she worked, doing the family washing, when she saw an Indian approaching.

"Go away," she ordered when he came near.

She was very busy and did not want to be bothered. But he did not pay any attention to her words and stood there watching her for a while,

This was exasperating to Melinda, so finally she picked up a stick of stove wood which was nearby, thinking she might frighten him away. She threw it at the Indian, and to the apparent surprise of both of them, it knocked the man down!

"Heap spunky squaw," the fellow remarked, as he got up. Then he went on his way.

Council Bluffs was founded about twenty years before Melissa went there to begin working. At first it had been a Mormon settlement called Kanesville, and a part of the town was still predominantly Mormon. Melissa worked for a while in the home of a Mormon family where the lady of the house assumed the role of an invalid. The city derived its later name from the council held on the bluffs between the Indians and the early explorers, Lewis and Clark.

About two years after Melissa started working in Council Bluffs, her grandfather brought her ten-year-old brother Robert in for a farewell visit. They came with team and wagon, and Grandfather came up to the house where she was working, but Bobby had become shy, so she went out to the wagon to talk with him. Of course, she was happy to see them, but sad to learn that they were going to move away.

She learned that her grandparents had decided to move further west, to Colorado, and of course her brother was going along with them, but the rest of the children would remain where they were In Iowa.

Colorado seemed a long distance away then, and this was the last time Melissa ever saw the little brother who had meant so much to her as a playmate during her early childhood years. She did not see her grandparents again either.

Since Melissa was only twelve years old, a guardian was appointed to look out for her after her grandparents left Iowa. Aunt Mary's husband was chosen to fill this position, and since he and Aunt Mary lived across the Missouri River in the state of Nebraska, this meant that the orphan girl would also be leaving Iowa soon if she was taken to live with them.

When the Mormons had arrived at the Missouri River on their way west in 1846, they built settlements on both sides of the river and stayed through the winter months. On the Nebraska side of the river, their village was later developed into a town known as Florence, and it was here that the Lingner family lived. Nebraska became a state only a short time before Melissa went to Florence to live with her aunt and uncle.

It was really Aunt Mary who took charge of her orphaned niece, and it seemed to Melissa that she was required to work awfully hard, and her aunt was very cross with her. On one occasion she was helping her uncle outside. They were working in the garden when his hat blew off and frightened the horse he was using, so they nearly had a runaway. From this incident it is evident that she helped outdoors as well as inside.

Uncle Lingner was a spiritualist medium, and often held séances for people who wanted to ask questions of the spirits. Melissa did not know much about spiritism at that time, but she thought it was something evil and the work of the devil.

Sometimes when her uncle sought information from the spirits, he was thrown about and treated so roughly by them that he was exhausted afterward from it all. These "fits," as they were called, frightened Melissa, and because of this rough treatment from the spirits, Uncle Lingner later gave up his dealings with the spirits altogether.

Chapter 4

A Home of Her Own

Aunt Mary and Uncle Lingner soon decided that Melissa should be "hired out" to work for wages. They knew the girl's past experience had been good training for such work, and now she was old enough and strong enough to work on a job which would not only provide her with room and board but bring in some money besides. So Aunt Mary found such a job for her niece at Mrs. Arnold's hotel.

This was quite different from helping in private homes where she took care of children, did family washings, and helped with other family tasks around the home. Here she had much heavier work, and often worked longer hours. She had to be up early and sometimes had to work late at night to finish the tasks assigned to her for the day. One of the hardest parts of her work while at the hotel was doing the big washings. She had to carry all of the necessary water from a well outside the building, and all the hotel linens had to be washed. She often wished that she might have been allowed to stay in Council Bluffs.

The money she earned was all collected by her aunt, so Melissa did not have any of her wages to spend. The only time she ever received any of the money she earned while working at the hotel was one time when her aunt gave her two dollars to buy a pair of shoes for herself.

Just after her fourteenth birthday, Melissa was brought back to live with her aunt and uncle. Aunt Mary had decided to take in roomers, so it would be to their advantage to have Melissa working for them. She soon had all the work she could do cleaning rooms and doing washings for the people who stayed at Lingner's Rooming House, as well as helping in the kitchen.

At one time, a number of Norwegian men who worked on the railroad were staying in the rooming house, and they wore very long, heavy woolen shirts—so long they reached nearly to their knees. These shirts were, of course, very hard to wash.

One of these men, a big fellow much older than Melissa, took a liking to her, and evidently made up his mind that she would make a good wife for him. But "Lizzie," as everyone called her, did not at first notice this fellow's interest in her.

"It's no wonder that fellow would like to have our Lizzie," Aunt Mary remarked to her husband. "She is a good girl, knows how to work, and is getting to be quite pretty."

One morning while Aunt Mary was braiding Melissa's hair, this man came into the kitchen where they were and stood watching.

"She's my girl," he said to Mrs. Lingner.

Melissa did not say anything, but she thought, *I am not!* most emphatically.

After that she tried to avoid him as much as she could, but of course, this was not easy because they were living in the same house. She had no place in her life and plans for such a man as this, and she certainly did not want to go on washing those heavy shirts all her life!

During the summer, after her work for the day was finished, Melissa sometimes went for a walk in the evening. She liked to walk along the river or sit on the bank to rest. After one particularly warm and tiring day, she thought it would be nice and cool by the river, so she sat on the bank to rest. She did not go unobserved, however.

Out by the river, Melissa had just settled herself for a refreshing rest, when suddenly her admirer appeared beside her and sat down too.

"Lizzie, will you marry me?" were his first words.

Without acknowledging his presence, or answering him a word, she got up and made a beeline straight back to her aunt's home. She was very much relieved when these men left the rooming house a short time later and moved on to another location as the railroad progressed.

In the fall of 1869, a family, traveling through on their way to California, stopped in Florence at the rooming house. They were traveling in covered wagons and had come from Missouri. Deciding to spend the winter in Florence, they stayed at the rooming house until they could find a suitable house to rent.

David and Lydia Pettegrew had seven children, ranging in age from baby Charles, about two years old, to the eldest son, who was twenty-five. Between them there were five girls: Caroline, Harriet, Lucinda, Dora, and Mary.

When Melissa saw this family, she recognized the oldest son as the "young knight who came riding on a white horse," and stayed overnight at her grandfather's home about five years earlier. He was Alden Pettegrew, whom her grandfather had called a "remarkable young feller" because of his honesty in paying for the night's lodging.

David Pettegrew had been to California twenty years before this. When Alden and his sister Carrie were just tiny tots, and the family lived in Iowa, their father caught "gold fever" and became one of the "forty-niners."

"While on my way to the California gold fields, one of my oxen just laid down on the desert and wouldn't go any further," Mr. Pettegrew related. "It was so hot and it had been so long since we had had any water to drink that he was no longer able to keep going. We were near enough to water then that I was able to go on and get some for him, but he would not drink it. He just laid there and died.

"Then I took the other one to the river so he could drink, but he walked into the water and just stood there. Oxen are smart enough not to drink a lot of water when they are overheated. He went into the water and stood there to cool off before he would begin to drink any of it."

Although Mr. Pettegrew was lucky enough to reach California alive, he did not have any luck in his search for gold, so he finally decided to return to Iowa. His family had begun to fear that he, too, had died along the way; it was so long before he returned.

This time Mr. Pettegrew was not interested in searching for the elusive gold, but he intended to secure land in California for a home.

When Melissa saw this family, she recognized the oldest son as the "young knight who came riding on a white horse," and stayed overnight at her grandfather's home about five years earlier.

Having the Pettegrew family at the rooming house made life much more pleasant for Melissa. Hattie was just a few months older than Melissa, and the two girls soon became good friends. With Carrie, the older sister, they formed a threesome, going about almost everywhere together. Of course, Melissa had to work, and was not free to go with the other girls at all times, but usually she could go.

While staying at the rooming house, Mr. Pettegrew heard talk about homesteads still available in eastern Nebraska, and he became interested in the idea of homesteading. Alden, too, was interested, so they set out together in search of homestead land. They found country to their liking in Dodge County, northwest of Florence, and there they each filed claim on an eighty-acre piece of land.

After Alden and his father returned to Florence from this trip, the family moved into a house which they rented. It was not far from the rooming house, and they planned to spend the winter months there but would move onto the homesteads early the next spring.

The friendship between Melissa and the two older Pettegrew girls was continued after the move the same as before. The three girls enjoyed going most everywhere together, often just for a walk along the river when the weather permitted.

It was usually in the early evening when they went walking together, and during these walks they could talk over things of mutual interest without interruption. Sometimes Alden would join the girls as they started out to go for a walk.

On one of these occasions Melissa was wearing a new dress, which made it a special event for her, because new clothes were something rare in her young life. The hem in this new gingham dress was sewed in a chain stitch, and while they were walking, the thread caught on a weed or twig along the way and was broken. Before Melissa realized what was happening, the hem had come completely out of her nice, new dress, and there was nothing to do but return home at once.

More and more, as time went by, the threesome became a foursome. Alden was a rather shy young man, but his admiration for the pretty orphan girl was growing every day. She was happy to have his sisters for her friends and was not thinking much about romance yet, so it was awhile before she realized that his presence with the group was specifically because of her.

The Pettegrew girls did not like the nickname "Lizzie" any better than Melissa herself did, although that was what most everyone called her, so they initiated a campaign to change her name. "May" was the name chosen and used by Carrie and Hattie. They refused to call her Lizzie at all.

After the family left the rooming house, Alden continued to keep his horses in Lingner's barn, so he was often there to feed and water them, clean the stables, and take them out for exercise.

One of Melissa's tasks was to get the milk each morning. On cold, wintry mornings she would throw a shawl over her head and go down the street past where the Pettegrew family lived, after the milk. On her return journey she would often find that Alden had joined her on his way to tend to his horses in the Lingner barn. However, instead of walking beside her as most young men would do, he walked just a bit behind, or let her keep just a step ahead of him, as if in deference, or because of shyness.

The four young friends all liked to sing, so they enjoyed going to any social events where there would be singing. They went to church together and to other community events such as parties and dances. Melissa liked to dance, but Alden did not care to dance very much.

Alden and Melissa also attended night school together for a while that winter. She was pleased to have such a nice young man for a friend, and to know he came from a good family, all of whom she knew and liked very well, so she did not try to avoid him as she had that other fellow.

When he called at the Lingner home, however, Aunt Mary had to do most of the talking, because he was such a quiet young man. Sometimes he brought gifts of fruit or candy for Melissa.

Would any of the Pettegrew family go on to California later on? Someone wondered about this and had Uncle Lingner ask the question of the spirits during one of his séances. The answer was given that all of them, except one, would later see California.

The friendship between Alden and Melissa May grew and developed from mutual admiration into true affection and love. He began thinking more about the future, as time marched on—a future which he hoped would include her. Finally he found the courage, when they were alone together one day, to ask her about it.

She awoke on the seventeenth day of March, 1870, in happy anticipation of a different and perhaps much better kind of life opening up just before her. It was her wedding day.

"May, will you marry me before we leave, and come with us to the homesteads as my wife?"

"I will if Uncle Lingner gives his consent," she replied. "He is my guardian you know, so I could not get married without his permission."

So Alden had to ask her uncle for her "hand in marriage." Uncle Lingner gave his consent to the marriage, although Aunt Mary would have much preferred keeping her niece as long as possible because of the work she was able to do for her in the rooming house.

They planned to be married just before leaving Florence.

The prospect of becoming a member of the Pettegrew family was a very pleasant one for the orphan girl. She felt that she would be an orphan no longer, and that Alden's parents, sisters, and brother would be the nicest kind of substitutes for her own lost and scattered loved ones.

There was no one willing or able to provide a new wedding outfit for the bride, so the old rhyme of "something old, something new, something borrowed, and something blue," was truly a fitting description. But this did not seriously mar Melissa May's happiness as she prepared for her wedding.

She awoke on the seventeenth day of March, 1870, in happy anticipation of a different and perhaps much better kind of life opening up just before her. It was her wedding day.

The marriage was performed by the Lutheran minister. Aunt Mary and Uncle Lingner went to the parsonage to witness the marriage, and all the Pettegrew family were there too. It was no brief ceremony like most are today, but the young couple had to stand for an hour while the minister read the lengthy ceremony.

On the following day they started on the journey to their homesteads in Dodge County. There were two wagons, and Father Pettegrew drove the lead wagon, in which most of the family rode. Alden followed, with May beside him, in the second wagon loaded mostly with household goods.

When the last "goodbye" was said, the orphan girl was indeed off on a new adventure, headed for a new life of experiences to be enacted on the rolling land of the Nebraska farm country. From this time on she was May Pettegrew. She had left behind her old name, all of it, as well as the loneliness of being a homeless orphan. The little scarred hands had grown strong and experienced. They were ready for whatever tasks and services there might be need for her to perform.

The afternoon brought signs of a coming storm, so the Pettegrew family continued as late as they could, for they wanted to go as far as possible before it struck. Finally they had to stop, as darkness was overtaking them, so they turned in at a farm home along the way, seeking shelter for the night.

To make room in his barn for their horses, the farmer took one of his young animals, a heifer, out of the barn and put her in a lean-to shed which was on one side of the main building. Then a rope was stretched from the barn to the house and fastened securely at both ends, so that no one would get lost while trying to go to and from the barn during the storm.

And storm it was. Their honeymoon trip was interrupted by a real Nebraska blizzard.

The next morning when the men went out to the barn to take care of their stock, they found the heifer in the lean-to had frozen to death during the night. The storm did not let up, but continued all that day and they were not able to resume their journey until three days later. Then they made their way through the snowdrifts to their homesteads.

Father Pettegrew's homestead had a frame house standing on it, built by someone previously living on the place, and left standing empty, so there was a place for the family to live when they arrived. It was for this reason they were able to move to the homestead so early. If there had been no buildings, the entire family could not have moved out until after some sort of shelter had been built.

Alden and May would not have a home of their own until sometime later, but since the two homesteads were adjoining, Alden could work his land, and as time and money permitted, build a house, while they lived with his parents.

It was a pretty location, a country of rolling hills covered with lots of grass. Dodge was one of the original eight counties organized in Nebraska. There were several towns in the area, the nearest one being North Bend, nine miles away. Scribner was ten or twelve miles distant, and Fremont, the county seat, was twenty miles away. These three towns formed sort of a triangle around the homesteads which the Pettegrews had taken.

It was the coming of the railroads which had brought about the settlement of the small towns scattered about this country. The Union Pacific Railroad had been completed, coast to coast, in 1869, and from that time on, short lines kept spreading like a net over the state. Before the railroads came, people had settled mostly along the Missouri River where water, timber, fish, and small game were more plentiful. The open prairie was exposed to blizzards, and susceptible to droughts, so was not at first very inviting, but railroads made provisions more easily obtainable.

The Indians of this area were of the Omaha tribe and were not troublesome except that they often came to the doors of the white man's homes to beg for food.

Alden and his parents knew that getting started in a new land would not be an easy task, but they were not afraid of hard work, and neither was May. To her it seemed that life was more pleasant and purposeful than it had ever been before. To be of service in a family group she could call her own, and who accepted her as one of them, meant so much to her who had spent so much of her life working for those who gave so little in return.

It was hard work to prepare new ground which had never been worked before, but crops were planted in as much of the land as they could get ready that first spring. A garden was also an important consideration, but it took time to grow vegetables, so often they had very little to eat during those early days on the homesteads.

The Pettegrew family had a cow, and it became one of May's tasks to do the milking and otherwise care for the source of this food supply. There were chickens to take care of also, for they had eggs to use, at least some of the time. A favorite supper dish, when they had little else, was made by thickening milk with eggs and flour as it was heated. This was called thickened milk.

The little creek which went through the homestead had fish in it, so they provided an occasional change in the family menu, which was very monotonous at times.

For May, things really got worse before they got better. She had only one dress, so when it was soiled, she had to wash it out in the evening, to have it clean and ready to wear the next day. And her shoes were soon worn out, so she had to go barefoot most of that first summer.

Then Alden got a job working on the railroad for a while, using his team, and earning four dollars a day. He bought a pair of shoes for May that fall, but they were just straight shoes, seeming to have no left or right to them, so she had a hard time breaking them in to wear after having gone without shoes for so long.

Alden managed to save enough money from his earnings to buy the needed lumber for building a small house on their homestead, and the work of constructing it began as soon as there was time not needed for other more necessary tasks.

Meanwhile, May continued to help in the family home, doing much of the same work that she had been doing in the homes of other people. She was always ready and willing to do anything and everything that she could for the family. She did mending and sewing and braided straw from which she made hats for all of them, as well as many daily tasks.

The new home was only a twelve-by-twelve cabin, located about half a mile from the family home. Since the land which Alden had chosen for his homestead was somewhat lower than that of his father's place, it was "up to Pa's" or "down to Alden's" when anyone spoke of going from one place to the other, and the road between the two homes was a road merely because of usage.

May had little with which to furnish and decorate her little home, but she used newspapers on the walls for wallpaper, and put her ingenuity to work in other ways to make the home as comfortable and pleasant as she could. Her furniture was mostly boxes at first—she used them for chairs and made a cupboard out of them.

Thus the first year passed, and they were able to move into their own home before it was over.

Alden set out some trees on his homestead: an orchard of fruit trees including apples, plums, peaches, and walnuts, and they also set out a maple grove. May had a garden of her own to take care of the second year, and she managed to have a few flowers near her little home too.

They had fenced off a pasture, and Alden had planted it to bluegrass by sowing it on top of the snow during the first winter. It sprouted and grew the next spring, so they had a good stand of bluegrass as a result.

They added new pieces of real furniture one by one as time went on—a bedstead, a factory-made stove, table, and chairs.

And then in January of 1872, their first baby was born, a girl. They named her Harriet Jeanette and called her Nettie. Now the young mother added a new piece of furniture of her own making—a cradle for the baby.

Chapter 5

New Adventures

What a change had been made in the life of the orphan girl during the last two years. A husband, a home, and a baby girl were now hers to love and care for. True, the home was very small and the furnishings were meager. The work was hard, too, but it was all being done with and for those she loved. True love can make any task more pleasant, any situation easier to handle, any burden less heavy to bear.

There were no church buildings out on the prairie, so the school houses were used to hold meetings in when the ministers of the various denominations came through. Although May did not have any definite religious affiliation, she did have a religious faith, and had acquired at least one definite idea from her own reading of God's Word.

The Pettegrew family belonged to the Methodist church, and May thought she would like to join it, too, but there was one thing which caused her to hesitate. She knew that, according to the Bible, the correct mode of baptism was by immersion, and felt that she would not feel truly baptized any other way.

In reading the story of Christ's baptism in the Jordan River, by John the Baptist, she had noted that "Jesus, when he was baptized, went up straightway out of the water" (Matt. 3:16). That didn't sound like mere sprinkling to her, for to come up out of the water, she reasoned that He would of necessity first have to go down into the water.

Further on she read of Philip baptizing the eunuch.

> And as they went on their way, they came unto a certain water: and the eunuch said, See, here is water; what doth hinder me to be baptized? And Philip said, If thou believest with all thine heart, thou mayest. And he answered and said, I believe that Jesus Christ is the Son of God. And he commanded the chariot to stand still: and they

went down both into the water, both Philip and the eunuch; and he baptized him. And when they were come up out of the water, the Spirit of the Lord caught away Philip, that the eunuch saw him no more: and he went on his way rejoicing. (Acts 8:36–39)

May had come to realize that baptism symbolized much more than just the washing away of sin, as some thought. To her it meant that "we are buried with him by baptism into death: that like as Christ was raised up from the dead by the glory of the Father, even so we also should walk in newness of life" (Rom. 6:4). Only baptism by immersion truly showed that one believed in Christ's death and resurrection.

"If the Methodist minister will baptize me that way, I will join the Methodist church," she told the family.

So when the minister came, he was asked about it.

"We do not believe that is necessary," he said.

"But that is the way people were baptized in New Testament times," May reminded him, "and that is the only way I will be baptized."

When he found out that she meant it, and would be baptized no other way, he admitted that Methodist ministers did use this form of baptism in cases where the candidates insisted upon it.

"If that is what you want, I will do it," he told her.

There were several others who were baptized by sprinkling at the same time, and joined the Methodists, but May was the only one among the group who followed her Lord's example by going all the way down into the water and coming up out of the water into "newness of life."

The little maple grove survived and grew, and so did many of the fruit trees. In Nebraska, largely an open state without trees, it was early seen necessary that something be done to increase its timber area. So the settlers usually planted trees, and the state adopted a resolution to appoint a day especially for tree planting. It was the first state in the Union to have such a day—Arbor Day. The first one was celebrated April 10, 1872.

As a young mother, May displayed her fair share of the well-known American ingenuity. When the weather grew warm, flies came, and she had to keep the baby's cradle covered with mosquito netting to keep them away from her while she slept. One evening she mentioned this to her husband.

"Yes, the flies are getting bad already this summer," he agreed, not knowing what she was planning to do.

"Well, I've been thinking of a better way to deal with them," May continued. "If I could fix mosquito netting for screens to put on the windows, and make a screen door of the netting, too, I could keep the flies out of the whole house. Don't you think I could do that?"

"Folks will laugh at you for that," Alden answered. "No one has anything like that around here."

"Maybe they don't, and maybe they will laugh, but I want to try it."

She was not discouraged by his words but went ahead with her plan. Soon she had made a framework door over which she stretched netting, as well as the frames for her windows also. Then the flies had to stay outside of her little house, unless they could sneak in when someone had the door open.

It was true—people did laugh at her for what she had done. That is, they did at first, but it was not long until some of them had followed her example, and the flies were screened out of their homes too.

> *The panic which swept the country added to their problems. It was scarcely worthwhile to haul crops to market.*

May did not have safety pins with which to fasten baby diapers—only straight pins were generally available then. The first modern safety pins were made by a New York man shortly before the Civil War, as a small business venture, but the modern safety pin industry was not established until sometime later, after 1872.

When baby Nettie was about six months old, she contracted scarlet fever and became very ill. In a short time, the grim reaper had her in his hands, and death had once more touched the orphan girl's life. Sorrowfully the young couple buried their firstborn in one corner of the homestead, but they missed her badly, even though they had a busy life with no time to sit and mourn over the hard experiences that came their way.

The following year was a hard one for the farmers who were not yet well established on the Nebraska prairie. It was the worst one in the experience of most of the older settlers as well. Beginners had as yet no reserve supplies stored up against years of crop failure, and this year there was a drought. In an agricultural country such as this, the results of a drought were felt almost at once.

The panic which swept the entire country that year only added to their problems. Prices went so low that the crops which did come through the drought were almost valueless and it was scarcely worthwhile to haul them to market.

The main crop on the Pettegrew homesteads was corn, which they usually shelled and hauled to Scribner where it was sold for cash. Then they bought the things they needed but could not raise on the land or make themselves. The corncobs were used for fuel. But that winter the corn was so cheap it was often burned for fuel—corn on the cob—without bothering to shell the kernels off. It made a good hot fire too!

When Alden made a trip to Fremont with a load of corn, he could not afford to take a room there for the night because it would cost him almost as much as he was paid for his load of corn, and then there would not be enough money left for him to buy the things he needed to take home.

In some localities, farmers had other problems, too, that year. If a prairie fire or grasshoppers had taken their crops during the summer, they were even more discouraged, and many gave up and moved away. History tells of prices almost unbelievably low during that period—corn at ten cents a bushel, eggs five cents a dozen, and butter nineteen cents a pound.

Winter work was scarce, but Alden got a job working for a neighbor, Mr. Jones, for fifty cents a day. Mrs. Jones wanted May to work for her, but Alden's mother did not think it would be proper for the wife to work out, so May deferred to her mother-in-law's wishes, much as she would have liked to earn some money. So Alden's sister worked for Mrs. Jones instead.

Perhaps it was because she had known a mother's love so short a time, and afterward felt unwanted because no home was found for her, that May was especially anxious to please her husband's family. She wanted them to like her, but her interest in and concern for others did not end with the family, for she wanted to do good for all who needed help, at all times, and in all places. She was always ready and willing to go to the aid of anyone in time of sickness and sorrow, regardless of her own circumstances.

Early in 1874, May's second child was born, a boy. They named him Walter David, and she was happy again to have a baby in her arms. When the gardens and early crops were in and doing nicely, the future began to look brighter, and the farmers became hopeful again. But one fateful day late in June or early July something appeared like a great dark cloud in the sky, hiding the sun. It came in the afternoon and soon settled down over all the land.

Grasshoppers!

By the next morning there were no gardens; there were no early crops; there was no corn in the fields, just the bare stalks standing there. In one short afternoon the hopes of a whole year were gone.

"After the hoppers ate up everything green, they sat on the fence, spitting tobacco juice," Father Pettegrew said afterward.

Yes, the pests had eaten his tobacco crop too!

Those who have never seen one of these grasshopper raids cannot realize what they were like. The ground and all vegetation seemed alive and crawling with life. While they remained, everything was hidden by them, and when they moved on, nothing was left above the ground in the fields and the gardens except perhaps the stalks which they could not eat.

May felt like weeping for the loss of all which had made them feel so hopeful only a few hours before. Their only food crop which really escaped the grasshoppers that year was onions. That fall they stored onions upstairs in Alden's parents' home, where, during the winter evenings after they went up to bed, Alden's sisters often ate onions, just as one might eat apples, and they enjoyed them too!

As a result of this grasshopper plague following so soon after the troubles of the previous year, many people in Nebraska became dependent, and had to have help with food and clothing through the winter, as well as seed to plant for a new start the next spring.

That winter there were no corncobs for fuel, and little money to buy coal, so Alden gathered the cornstalks which were still standing in his fields and cut them into stove-wood lengths. He would fill a ten-bushel bin after he came home from work in the evening, and it would last long enough to keep a fire that evening, and the next morning there was enough to last while May prepared breakfast. Then the supply had to be replenished.

It was a winter of deep depression, little work, almost no money, and not much to eat. Figure-four traps, consisting of a trigger and a box-like frame covered with wire netting, were baited and set to catch the prairie chickens or sage hens. These helped to vary their diet, and sometimes May sold some of the dressed hens.

The grasshoppers had flown away before cold weather came, but they left eggs behind them, in the ground, ready to hatch into young hoppers in the spring. Certainly that was a depressing thought.

The spring of 1875 finally came—another chance to plow, plant, plan, and hope. The young grasshoppers hatched from the eggs and began eating the early crops, but soon they flew on to "greener pastures," so all the later crops were saved. They had something to show for all their hard work that year.

Alden accepted a cow in payment for some work he did for someone, so May took on the chore of caring for their cow, and whenever she could, she made butter to sell. On one occasion she had several pounds of butter made up and ready for sale when she learned that Father Pettegrew was going to town, so she sent it with him. Each pound was not wrapped separately in the sanitary method of a later day, but she had the container covered with a clean cloth. Somehow, on the way to town, the cloth became loosened and was blown off, so it was covered with dirt when Father Pettegrew arrived at his destination and was not saleable. May was much disappointed when he returned with the butter instead of the money which she had been counting on. She had planned just how she would spend that money, and to her, the most important item on her list was a gift for her mother-in-law.

Another baby boy, Alden and May's third child, arrived on March 20, 1876, and they named him Ernest Jackson.

That spring, May and Hattie, Alden's sister, working together, planted ten acres of corn. May used an ax to cut an opening in the sod, and Hattie, following behind her, dropped the seed into the opening, then pressed the sod together again by stepping on it after the ax was removed. Then they changed places for a while, with Hattie using the ax to cut the sod, while May did the planting. It was very tiresome work, but they kept at it, alternating the work so it would not become so tiring, until they had the ten-acre field all planted.

May often sang as she sat rocking the baby in the cradle with one foot. Lullabies such as "The Sweet little Robin," "Rock-a-Bye Baby," and other little songs that she knew were always enjoyed by Walter, as well as helping to quiet the baby into sleep. Meanwhile her hands were almost always busy with mending, sewing, or whatever else she might do with her hands.

Some of those times she read the Bible or some other of the few books or papers available. They did not have many books, but those they did have were well read.

One evening as May was sitting with the Bible in her hands, reading again those "ten great words" in Exodus 20, she paused thoughtfully and seemed to be puzzled about something.

"Alden, the Bible says that the seventh day is the Sabbath. I suppose Sunday must be the seventh day then, or everyone would not be keeping it as they do."

But Alden did not agree with her conclusion.

"No," he told her, "Sunday is not the seventh day."

"But—"

"You just take a look at the calendar over there hanging on the wall, and you can see that Sunday is the first day of the week."

"Oh, yes, of course it is," she agreed. "But then, why is it that we observe a different day of rest now than was observed in Bible times? I don't understand that, do you?"

"No, I don't understand it either, but that's the way it is."

Finding that he knew no more about it than she did, May went back to her reading, still puzzled about the matter but not knowing how she could get any more information. Although she did not mention the subject again, neither did she forget it altogether. Instead, she hoped that someday she might find the answer.

Six years had passed since they came to the homestead. There had been many discouragements, but somehow they had managed to stay on, to stick with their land, and even make some improvements on it. An addition had been built onto the little house, so now May had more room in which to do her housekeeping.

Besides keeping those two rooms neat and homelike, and taking good care of her two little boys, she always took care of the garden. In it a variety of vegetables were grown for table use and some to store for later needs. There were flowers blooming, in season, near her door: usually moss roses and four o'clocks were among them.

Another year brought increased rainfall, and still better times seemed to be ahead for the settlers. Because crops were better and prices improved, they were encouraged to plan for more and larger improvements on the homestead.

Walter liked to follow his mother wherever she went as she worked outside the house, and as soon as the baby was able to walk well enough, she had two little followers. They played together nearby as she worked, or watched as she fed the chickens, took care of the animals, and worked in the garden. Sometimes they tried to do the same things she was doing.

Like most farmers, Alden raised hogs, and some of the corn he raised was used to feed them. They were kept in a large pen north of the cattle shed, but there was a lane for the hogs to go through from the pen to the hog wallow, and a long wooden trough reached from the well to this wallow so the water could be poured into the trough as it was drawn from the well.

May and the little boys were there one day, and after the water stopped running, Ernest was attracted by the drops still falling from the end of the trough. He started trying to catch them in his mouth, and while doing this, suddenly lost his balance and fell flat on his face in the muddy wallow.

Walter laughed at the sight, but his mother did not. She promptly reached over the mud and fished the little fellow out by grasping his clothing in the center of his back and lifting him up. This, too, was amusing to Walter, for Ernest struggled in his mother's grasp, and spattered mud all around during the rescue operation.

"Why, Walter!" May said reprovingly, "don't you know that your little brother might have been drowned in the mud? Then you would not have him to play with anymore."

This thought startled the older boy, and he sobered immediately, as if it struck him with awesome force. He had not realized that Ernest might have been suffocated in the hog wallow if his mother had not rescued him at once. Walter was a loving child and did not want to have his baby brother harmed in any way.

The two little boys were very dear to their mother, but by now May had begun to wonder if her family was going to be all boys. She longed for a little girl, and this heart's desire was realized in 1878 when on January 14, their fourth child was born, a daughter whom they named Lydia Grace.

Alden had some wheat stored in a bin built into one corner of the living room, because there had not been room anywhere else to store it. One evening while he was up to his parent's home and the three children were all asleep, May started to work putting the wheat into sacks.

As she worked, she thought she felt something touch her back, but she did not pay any attention to it at first. The second time it happened, she wondered if someone had touched her, and turned around to see if Alden might have returned and slipped up behind her to surprise her, but no one was there.

Because she was alone, except for the sleeping children, she began to feel just a little frightened, so when she felt the touch the third time, she screamed. Then suddenly she realized what it was, and quickly got rid of it. Her work with the wheat had disturbed a mouse!

When May went to town with Alden, she often left Walter with Mother Pettegrew while she was away. Grandmother became very fond of the little boy and enjoyed talking with him.

"Grandma and Grandpa are growing old," she said to him on one of these occasions. "Someday we will not be able to do things like we can now. Maybe then we will need someone to take care of us."

This touched Walter's sympathetic nature, so he said, "When I grow up, Grandma, I'll take care of you and Grandpa."

"That would be nice. But your mother and father will be growing old, too, and who will take care of them?"

"Oh, Ernest will take care of them," was the prompt reply.

Alden's two oldest sisters were now married and living in their own homes. Hattie married a widower, Frank Plantz, who had three children, and she had one of her own, too, now. Carrie, who had been the first to marry, was now Mrs. Matthew Roberts, and lived on a farm about two miles away.

Carrie and Matt had no children of their own, but they had taken an orphan girl into their home. Her name was Hattie. One day when Carrie and little Hattie were visiting May, some trouble developed between the little girl and Ernest while they were playing in the front yard.

May had always taught her children to tell the truth, but the orphan girl now playing with her children had not been taught to be truthful before she came to live with Carrie.

There were some flowers growing in the yard where the children were, and Ernest pulled some of them up. Then the quarreling started, and Carrie went out to see what the trouble was all about.

Hattie told her that Ernest had pulled up the flowers, but Ernest said Hattie was the one who had pulled them up. Having more faith in Ernest's word than she had in the girl, Carrie gave Hattie a whipping. But she noted that Ernest seemed to be a little too pleased about this, so she started talking with him, telling him how bad it was to tell something that was not true. Suddenly Ernest began to cry and admitted that he had been the one to pull up the plants.

At this point May came out, and she gave Ernest a hard whipping, making it very clear to him that the punishment was for not telling the truth and for causing Hattie to be punished for what he had done.

Never again did May have any trouble with Ernest not telling the truth.

Chapter 6

Better Times

May persisted in her use of family names for her children, especially names from her husband's family. When their fifth child, another daughter, was born on May 12, 1880, she was named Suwano Elizabeth. How the Indian name Suwano came to be used by the Pettegrew family is not known, but Alden's sister Suwano had not lived to maturity.

Walter was six years old now, and he began attending school in the fall. It was about a mile from the homestead to the Webster school, where a small store and post office were also located.

The next year, during a diphtheria epidemic, Walter became ill, and May suspected that he had the dreaded sickness. Their nearest neighbor, Mrs. Adams, came over to visit, with her children, but May went out to meet her, and warned her that she feared Walter had diphtheria, and perhaps they should not come in.

"I am not afraid," Mrs. Adams told her, and came into the house with her children. Like many others, she seemed to feel that children might as well get the contagious diseases and have them over with.

It was diphtheria.

Walter grew steadily worse, until he refused to eat anything at all, because his throat hurt so badly. One night as May sat by the boy's bed, she fell asleep, and in her dreams, she saw a hand at the window beckoning to her sick boy. After that she felt sure that he would not pull through and was thus somewhat prepared for it when the end finally came.

During an epidemic like this, many children died; families would often lose from one to all of their children within a short period of time. It was said that one family of six children all became ill, and every one of them died.

The Adams children did not escape—they all came down with diphtheria, and one of them died.

Walter's death was a real blow to the entire family. Grandmother said she thought he surely was taken right to heaven because he was such a good little boy, perhaps too good to go on living here below. Sorrowfully they buried him beside his sister in the southwest corner of the homestead.

May went out where Alden was working near the house one pleasant summer day, leaving the children inside. "The baby is asleep," she told him, "and I told Ernest and Lydia to stay inside until I return. I'm going to Mrs. Adams' house for a little while."

"All right," he said. "I will be nearby until you get back."

But the two children who were inside the house soon grew restless and forgot about the baby.

> *"See how the fire burns the grass, Lydie," Ernest was saying as he held a lighted match to the dry grass and weeds at his feet. Then, looking up, he saw his father starting toward them from the house.*

"I'm tired of playing in here," Ernest said. "I'm going outside. Come on, let's go make a playhouse. I'll get some matches to burn off the grass."

"Make a fire?" Lydia asked.

"Just a little fire. We'll burn off a clearing for a playhouse," he explained as he got the matches.

So out they went, not noticing that the baby was waking up, nor did they hear her crying after they left, so intent were they on their own purposes. Alden soon heard the crying baby and went into the house to see what was wrong. Finding the older children were not taking care of her as they were supposed to be doing, he came out, picked up a switch, and started to look for them.

"See how the fire burns the grass, Lydie," Ernest was saying as he held a lighted match to the dry grass and weeds at his feet. Then, looking up, he saw his father starting toward them from the house.

"Here comes Pa! I'll step on the fire and put it out," he said, and this is what he did. Then they both went to meet their father, who only scolded them for having left the baby alone in the house and sent them back in. He did not come near enough to where they had been playing to notice the blackened place which their little fire had left.

Because of the interruption, they hadn't satisfied their desire to "play with fire," so at another time when they did not have the responsibility of watching the baby or staying in the house, they went further out, and decided to burn off a place where the weeds were high near a stack of millet hay close by the stables. Here their little fire started burning its way right toward the haystack and they became frightened. They had to work as hard and fast as they could to put it out and prevent it from growing into a big fire, but they succeeded, and this experience taught them not to play with fire anymore because it was too dangerous.

Mother May later noticed both places where the little fires had been started, and she wondered about them, but did not learn the truth about what had happened until years later.

Ernest and Lydia often enjoyed playing in the hayloft. There they sometimes made tunnels in the hay through which they could crawl and caves in which to hide.

In July of 1882, May's sixth baby was born, a fair-haired girl whom they named Dora Adelaide. Suwano, who had dark hair and dark brown eyes, was no longer the youngest one in the family.

Soon after Dora's birth, Hattie and her children came to stay with Alden and May. Hattie was expecting her second child. The little home was very crowded, but beds were made on the floor, and there seemed to be room for all. When her baby arrived, a boy whom she named Charles, the total number of children in the little home came to nine!

There was always work to be done, and no time to be idle, whether there were nine children in the home, or only one. May was always busy, but housework and the care of her children were only part of the work she did. She helped in planting the crops, and she helped in the harvesting, as well as working in the garden and doing chores. When she was not working outside, or busy with the duties of her home and children, she would be busy sewing. A sewing machine became one of her first acquisitions above the necessities of life, and soon she began doing sewing for others to earn extra money, as well as doing the family sewing.

Because of the style in women's clothing in those days, dressmaking was not a simple task. Hoops and bustles were often worn, and many yards of material went into the making of some of the dresses. During those years on the Nebraska homestead, May learned to make most everything that people wore, and without instruction, in the school of experience. She became an expert dressmaker. Besides clothes for the children and women, she knew how to make men's coats and suits and clothing of all kinds for special occasions such as shrouds for burial and wedding dresses, etc.

She might have become a professional dressmaker in other circumstances, but out on the prairie, there was not opportunity enough for it as a specialty, and there were opportunities for many other things, so her talents were developed in other directions as well as this one because of her ingenuity and willingness to learn and do.

Alden's sister, Mary, came down with the measles while teaching school away from home, so she returned, expecting to go back to her work as soon as she was well again. But her father was anxious for her to marry, and so also was the man who wished to marry her, Mr. Townsend. She was persuaded to marry instead of returning to teaching, but her health was not very good, and she became very ill with dropsy not long after her marriage.

May was ever ready and willing to go to the aid of the sick and suffering, and she was the one who took care of her sister-in-law more than anyone else, for the Townsend home was nearby. After several weeks of suffering, Mary passed away, and they buried her in the little graveyard beside May's two children who had gone before.

Now it became evident which one of the Pettegrew family would never reach California—at least Mary never would. The spirits had revealed to Uncle Lingner that one of the family would never reach California.

Spelling bees, programs of various kinds, and all sorts of meetings were held in the schoolhouse, for there were no other public buildings where such gatherings could be held. Preparing to attend one of these, Alden called to May as he went out the door: "Are you about ready? I'm going to get the horse hitched up."

"We'll be ready by the time you get the buckboard here," May answered. A buckboard was a light four-wheeled vehicle which had a long elastic board, instead of a body and springs, resting directly on the bolster, and the seat was placed on this board.

The children were outside waiting when Alden drove up to the house. May came out, followed by the schoolteacher, who was boarding with them at the time.

"I'll walk, and you can drive the horse," Alden said as he climbed out and handed the reins to his wife. Miss Rankin and the girls piled onto the seat beside May, while Ernest rode behind it.

When the meeting in the schoolhouse was over, and they were ready to leave, they resumed their places in the buckboard and started for home. Alden and another man, Mr. Forney, walked down the road behind them.

As soon as they were on their way, May sensed that something was wrong. They seemed to be going faster and faster, and although she pulled harder and harder on the reins, she could not check the horse's speed.

"Ma! I'm out! Ma, I'm out!" She heard Ernest's voice calling from somewhere behind them as the horse was finally slowing down. They stopped and Ernest came running to climb in again.

"I fell out," he told them, breathlessly.

"Yes, we know. But you're not hurt, are you?" his mother asked.

"No, I guess not."

Alden and Mr. Forney caught up with them before they started on and found that the bit had somehow come out of the horse's mouth and fallen down across its neck, presumably while they were in the schoolhouse. That was why pulling on the reins did not seem to do any good. They were thankful that their brief runaway had been no more serious.

The welcome warmth of their little home enveloped Alden when he came in from work on a cold day. It was dinnertime. Taking off his heavy coat and scarf, he washed and sat down with his family to the good, hot mid-day meal which May had prepared.

After the meal was eaten, and the dishes partly stacked near one end of the table, they sat talking and resting for a while before going back to work. Suwano was not interested in the conversation, so she left the table and began looking for something to do. Alden had left his heavy scarf hanging on the back of a chair. Wannie, as the other children called Suwano because they found her name difficult to pronounce correctly, saw the scarf, and decided that it would make a good swing for her. She carefully tied one end of the scarf to the back of the chair, and then, looking around for some way to secure the other end, her glance fell upon the stack of plates on the table. So she laid the loose end of the scarf on the table and moved the plates onto it.

No one seemed to notice what she was doing, so there was no one to stop her before she tried to sit down in her nice new swing!

The crash which followed, however, brought the little brown-eyed girl into the limelight. The attention of all who had ignored her actions suddenly came to bear upon her, and she was frightened both by the results of her bright idea and the sudden attention. May did not punish the little girl, but she tried to explain to her just why she should not do things like that. She thought the accident itself had probably taught Wannie as much or more than any further punishment would.

Spring returned again, and when the weather was warm, May would often have the door open. She laid a chair across the open doorway to keep the baby inside, for Dora was crawling all about the house now.

"You girls stay in here with the baby," she told Lydia and Suwano, "while I am working outside." She took Ernest with her and they went off to their tasks.

While they were away, an Indian came walking toward the house. As he neared the door, the girls saw him coming. Lydia quickly ran out of sight into the next room. Suwano turned to see where her big sister was going, and then followed her into the adjoining room just in time to see her crawling under the bed and motioning as she crawled for Suwano to follow her.

Wannie started to join her sister in hiding, when suddenly she thought of little Dora all alone out there by the door with an Indian so near. She got up and went back into the other room to see what had happened, and to bring the baby back with her if she could.

She found that Dora had pulled herself up by the chair, and was standing there alone, looking out. But no Indian was anywhere in sight.

As soon as he realized that no adults were at the house, the Indian had gone on to the barn where May and her son were busy at work shelling corn with the hand sheller.

In the fall, a large horse-operated sheller was brought through the community to shell the main crop of corn, just as threshing machines did for the wheat and other grain crops at harvest time. But this was not the harvesting season yet, and they were shelling some corn which had been left over on the cob since the previous harvest.

"*Cheek-ee one*," said the Indian, as he approached them, holding up one finger. This meant he wanted them to give him a chicken. May let him have a chicken.

Then he became fascinated with the corn-sheller and turned it awhile, very rapidly, until he tired of the new toy, like a child, and was ready to stop.

Indians were quite troublesome in the area, coming often to the homes to beg for things, mostly food. Other than this, there was no serious trouble and had not been since the Pettegrews had been living here. Further west there were still some uprisings among the Indians.

On another occasion, an Indian came begging at May's door for something to eat early in the day. She fed him and he ate a hearty meal. What May did not know was that this fellow had just come from Mother Pettegrew's home where he had eaten a hearty breakfast also, and both women learned later that all the while he was in their homes, eating those two breakfasts, he was carrying a chicken under his blanket which he had probably been given by someone else where he stopped to beg before coming to their homes.

Alden returned from a trip to town one evening, bringing a little red rocking chair with him for Suwano. Of course, she thought it was wonderful—but Lydia was sadly disappointed because she did not get one too!

"That is not right, Pa," May told her husband, "to get Suwano a rocker, and not one for Lydia too." So the next time he went to town he brought back a little brown rocking chair for Lydia when he returned.

"I think my brown rocker is the prettiest," Lydia announced.

"I think my red rocker is the prettiest," Suwano responded.

So both of the girls were happy now, and May was happy too, enjoying the sight of her two little daughters so contentedly sitting side by side in their rocking chairs, as they often did, each with a hand on the other one's chair, rocking and rocking them together.

Ernest sometimes made toy boats for his own enjoyment, sailing them in the watering trough where the farm stock were watered. He made himself a popgun, too, but he shot Wannie in the eye with it one time, and so was deprived of his gun for punishment.

Suwano was easily frightened by listening to scary stories, and Lydia liked to frighten her, as well as make herself afraid too, by telling such fearful tales as she could imagine. They had overheard talk among their elders about a recent mad dog scare, so they were almost too scared to go outdoors, for fear a mad dog might come along.

The corn-sheller had come and gone that fall, leaving behind a huge pile of corncobs which was now being used for the family fuel supply. While Suwano was out gathering up corncobs to take into the house, she suddenly thought she saw a dog—or at least the dog's tail as the dog went around out of sight. She dropped the corncobs she had picked up and ran into the house as fast as she could.

"Mad dog out there," she said breathlessly as she came in the door. May was not at home, but Lydia was, so she closed the door and locked it.

They sat looking out the window for a while, but this was soon too dull for Lydia, so she began imagining things to frighten herself and Suwano even more. In the window glass she saw a crack which extended across one of the small panes and had spread apart enough so that a bug, perhaps a small fly, might have crawled through. This gave her an idea, and she enlarged the imaginary insect which could crawl in until by the time she had it through and on the inside of the window, in her story, it was a wolf.

They left their chair near the window and moved toward the center of the room.

Next, Lydia said she heard a noise coming from under the floor, and, to get away from that area, they both climbed up onto the table in the center of the room. There Mother May found them when she came in from working somewhere outdoors.

"What are you girls doing on the table?" she asked. "You know that is no place for you to be."

"We were 'fraid," they told her, and then she realized what had been going on. Explaining that there were many better things for them to think about, May told them not to think up such make-believe stories to frighten themselves anymore.

When baby Dora became ill with dysentery, May remembered that she had come in from working outside, all tired and warm, just before nursing the baby one day, so she thought this had probably been what started the illness. Babies were not bottle-fed unless it was really necessary.

The doctor thought the dysentery might be checked if May would stop nursing the baby, and feed Dora with a bottle, so the doctor's instructions were followed, or rather, May tried to follow the instructions, but little Dora would accept no nourishment at all from a bottle, and she grew steadily weaker.

Sometimes it is hard to know what might be the best thing to do. After the baby died, May wondered if she might not have been able to save her life if she had refused to follow the doctor's orders, but at the time she did not know what to do, and thought surely the doctor knew best.

So a new grave was dug in the southwest corner of the homestead, and now there were four in the little home cemetery. Sometime later, the caskets were all removed and placed in a cemetery away from the homestead where others were.

During that winter the teacher at the school was a man, Mr. Caskey. One afternoon he noticed a bad storm was coming up, perhaps a blizzard, so he dismissed the school, and took all the children to the home nearest to the school, which was the Adam's home. Leaving the children all there for fear some of them might get lost in the blizzard, which was soon raging over the prairie, he went on, stopping first at the Pettegrew home to tell them where Ernest was. Some of the children had quite a distance to go and could not have reached their homes before the storm made traveling very difficult.

At another school, in an adjacent community, the teacher also dismissed school early, but she let the children all go home by themselves. Two little girls, the Westphal sisters, started home like the others, but became lost in the storm before they could reach their home. The younger one got caught in the wire when they had tried to crawl through a fence, and they were too cold to get her free and go on, so the older one gave her coat to the younger, and both were found there after the storm was over, frozen to death.

Chapter 7

Alden's Disguise

"This summer, if all goes well, we are going to build a new house," Alden said to his wife one day in the spring of 1884. "I think it is about time to make some plans for a larger house."

"Then we can have a parlor, can't we?" May asked.

"Yes, we can have a parlor in our new house," he replied, smiling.

"And after that, I would like to have a parlor organ as soon as we can. We should have something better than my small accordion for music and for the children to learn to play."

The new house was built close by the grove, which was made up mostly of maple trees that Alden had set out just after they came to the homestead. It was a two-story building in an L-shape, and as soon as the work on it had progressed to the point where they could live in it, they moved in. It would be finished up inside as time went along.

Six rooms! After all the years of living in only two rooms, how May rejoiced in her new home! They all enjoyed its comparative spaciousness then, but in later years, when one by one, at various times, the older children returned to visit their childhood home, how very small it seemed to have grown with the passing of time.

They painted the new house white, and May planted a lawn of bluegrass, and of course she had flowers in the yard. For the inside, she made a rag carpet for the parlor, and they bought the little parlor organ she had hoped they could have. The children enjoyed gathering around it with their father to sing as May played a chord accompaniment, and each in turn, as they grew older, had opportunity to learn something about music.

May's sister, Kate, the one who had been brought up by the well-to-do family after their father's death, came to visit May's family in their new home. Kate was married and now lived in Denver, Colorado.

May was thirty years old that year, and the earliest known picture of her, a studio photograph of her and Alden together, was taken some time during the following winter.

On June 30, 1885, Mary Katherine, their seventh child was born. The woman who took care of May at this time had just lost a patient, so she became frightened when May told her that everything seemed to be turning black before her eyes.

She told Alden that his wife was dying but got some medicine from her medical kit, which seemed to help, and May was soon feeling better.

June was the month of Alden's birthday, as well as May's, so now there were three family birthdays in June.

Mother Pettegrew was anxious to take a trip to California to visit her sister, Sarah, who lived in Santa Cruz. The idea of this trip became even more inviting when Sarah came to Nebraska and wanted her sister to return with her to California. But there wasn't money to pay her way. Alden, too, became interested in going. He decided to finance the trip for himself and his mother by mortgaging his farm.

They went by train and stopped in Ogden, Utah, on the way to visit a brother who lived there, Alden's Uncle Elijah.

In California, Alden got work on a dairy farm to help with expenses and it was two or three months before he and his mother returned home. While he was away, his brother-in-law, Matt Roberts, sister Carrie's husband, took care of the farmwork on the homestead. Little Hattie stayed with Aunt May's family, too, because Carrie was away from home on a trip east to New York that summer. She went to visit her husband's relatives whom she had not met before.

While Alden and his mother were away, May often had Father Pettegrew down to her home for meals. Hattie and Lydia took turns with dishwashing, and they helped May take care of the new baby. Hattie especially enjoyed holding and carrying Mary around, as there were no younger children or babies in her homelife.

After the travelers returned that fall, Alden and May decided to buy a pony for the children to ride to school, for Lydia, too, was attending. The pony, Billy, proved to be so afraid of Indians that he would shake with fright whenever one came near.

Alden's sister, Dora, began teaching school that fall in North Bend.

"How is school teaching by now?" Alden asked when he saw her the first time after the beginning of the school term. "Have you had to spank any big boys yet?"

"No," she answered with a smile, "but I do have a baby to take care of."

Then she told them about one of her students, a little girl who was much too young to be attending school yet.

"I guess her mother was anxious to get her taken care of," she said. "I sent a note home to the mother asking her to please send the cradle."

"It just doesn't seem right to send children to school that young," May remarked. She wanted her children to get an education, but while they were babies, she wanted them with her at home.

Suwano was playing with some kittens near the barn one day while Ernest and Lydia were away at school. May came out of the house on her way to the neighbors, and seeing that Suwano was engrossed in play, thought she would not interrupt it to take her along, and that she would continue to be busy while she was away. Suwano did not know that her mother was gone, but she did stop playing soon and went into the house.

Not finding her mother anywhere in the house, she went outside again, not to play, but to look for her mother. Thinking she might have gone up to her grandmother's, Suwano struck out through the cornfield. The corn was so tall that she felt like she was in a forest, wandering around, but finally she came out where she could see her grandparent's home and went there.

Meanwhile, May had returned to the house. When she couldn't find Suwano, she looked around a bit, then found her tracks leading through the cornfield and followed them. When she arrived at Mother Pettegrew's home, Suwano came running to greet her as if she thought her mother had gone away for good; she was so glad to see her.

The unfinished upstairs in their new home made an ideal playroom for the children during the winter when they could not play outdoors very much. Ernest and Lydia put up a swing there.

"Come, Wannie, and we will push you in our swing," Lydia said to her after they had it all finished.

"No," she said, moving away from them.

"We'll get you then," and they started after her, intent on catching her so they could put her in the swing anyway, whether she wanted in or not. She ran around the chimney, with them following her.

"You go the other way," Lydia suggested to Ernest, "then we'll catch her."

He turned and cut off Suwano's way of escape, so she turned away from the chimney—but there was the open stairway right in her path. She fell all the way down, bumping on nearly every step.

The sound of someone bump-bumping down the stairs reached May's ever-alert ears, and she rushed into the room just in time to gather the little girl into her arms when she reached the last step. A search revealed no broken bones, but the fall had caused Suwano to bite the end of her tongue almost off, so she had a very sore tongue for a while.

"Ernest, you'll remember to draw the water, won't you?" May asked as she was climbing into the wagon to leave with Alden one day.

"Yes, Ma," he answered, and to be sure that he would not forget, he started to work right then as his parents were driving away.

Lydia, too, had some task to perform, but she insisted that Suwano had to help her. She started after her sister, who ran and climbed up on the corral fence.

"Leave her alone, Lydie," Ernest advised, "and do your work, so we will have time to play."

> *The sound of someone bump-bumping down the stairs reached May's ever-alert ears, and she rushed into the room just in time to gather the little girl into her arms when she reached the last step.*

This only irritated Lydia more, and she decided to try frightening the others into letting her have her own way.

"I'm going into the well then," she said, with a "nobody loves me" attitude. A box-like structure stood over the well, with the lid open while Ernest was drawing water from it by a bucket on the end of a long rope.

Lydia climbed into the box and stood on a very narrow strip inside the well, saying, "If I jump in, then you'll be sorry."

But Ernest kept on drawing water, although he was afraid she might fall in. He knew it would do no good to try to get her to come out, or to try to make her do so, for fear that she would fall in accidentally.

Finally, Lydia got tired of her little game, so she climbed out of the well box of her own accord.

When Alden and May heard about what Lydia had done, they talked it over and decided they must put a pump into the well. After the pump was installed, a permanent cover was built over the well opening so the children could not climb inside, nor accidentally fall into the well.

During the summer of 1886 they built a new barn. Brick was used in the foundation, and after it was hauled in and taken out of the wagon, May swept up all the brick dust from the bed of the wagon into a pan. She gave the pan to Suwano to take into the house, so they would have it for scouring the steel silverware and kettles.

"What do you have there?" Lydia asked when she saw her sister carrying the pan to the house.

"Just some brick dust," Suwano told her.

"Oh," Lydia paused speculatively, thinking that it was her turn to do the scouring in the morning. "Isn't that nice! Tell you what I'll do, Wannie. I'll let you be the first to use the nice new brick dust."

Lydia's little scheme worked, and the next day Suwano had the privilege of using the "nice new brick dust" first, while Lydia got out of her turn at doing the scouring.

Alden and May did not often attend the dances held in various homes of the community, because they did not want to keep the small children out late at night. But Alden's sisters and brother liked to dance and went as often as opportunity offered.

"We're going to have a dance at our house tonight," Sarah Adams told Lydia and Suwano one day while they were playing together. Sarah's sister, Maggie, was with her, and the four girls were near the Pettegrew home.

"Why don't you ask your mother if you can come over tonight, so you can watch the dancing," suggested Maggie.

Of course, Lydia and Suwano wanted to go, so they told May about it.

"Can we go, Ma?"

"Well, I guess you can go for a while," she told them. "But you must be home by bedtime."

"We will," they promised.

They thought it was great fun to watch the dancing, and afterward they added it to their repertoire of games. They remembered the bustles the girls wore at the dance, and remembered the man calling the dances, saying: "Bow to your partners," but they did not remember the exact words he used, so they said, "Bow your bustles to the men," when they played dancing.

The grove afforded a fine playground for the children. One cottonwood tree was taller than all the others, near the end of the grove, and some of the trees had grown so large that the girls could not reach around the trunks. May made syrup from the maple trees. They were not the real sugar maples, but the syrup was good. The trees would be tapped, and Ernest would go around collecting the juice that drained out and take it to the house for May to cook down into syrup.

Sunday school was held in the schoolhouse, but there was no local minister. A Methodist circuit rider came along occasionally, and whenever he came through the community, he held a meeting in the schoolhouse. The Pettegrews usually attended these meetings.

So many children were now attending the district school that there were too many for one teacher, and the schoolhouse was too small, but there was considerable disagreement among the people living in the district on the question of dividing it. A meeting was held at Alden's home to settle the problem, but some of those who did not want the district divided would not come to the meeting; they were so angry about it. Afterward it was divided, and a new schoolhouse built during the summer.

May enjoyed having company come to her home and was pleased when her sister Jennie and her daughter came to visit the family that summer. Kate was just about the same age as Suwano.

On baking day May usually gave Suwano a small piece of bread dough when she was getting ready to bake, for the little girl liked to pat it out flat and put it on the edge of the stove to bake. But this time, while Suwano went to get a knife to turn her dough over, cousin Kate took it and ate it up. That was when Suwano decided she did not like her cousin very well.

With the new schoolhouse only about half a mile from their home, the children did not need the pony anymore, and there were three of them to go now, for Suwano was six years old and started attending when the term opened in the fall. Mary was the only child at home while the others were in school, and as she was five years younger than Suwano, she had no one very near her own age with whom to share her toys.

When May's oldest sister, Melinda, came with her little son, Joe, for a visit, the two little children did not get along very well together. They both seemed to want the same things, and Mary was not willing to do very much sharing, so there was trouble.

The children were playing indoors one day and they all went into the bedroom, with baby Mary the last one to go in. She climbed onto the bed, and sat down, but the others all went back out before she could get down from the bed to follow them, and the last one out closed the door.

Suddenly Lydia realized that the baby had not come out.

"Mary's still in the bedroom, and the lamp is on the chair. She will get it," she said to Suwano. "We better go open the door."

They hurried to open the door, but by then Mary had reached it on the other side, so in opening the door, they knocked her flat onto the floor and were greeted by her screams.

She wasn't really hurt much, but her feelings were doubtless hurt more than a little for the way they had deserted her, shut the door, and then knocked her down. She cried so hard that Ernest became alarmed, so when she began holding her breath, he picked her up and rushed outside with her, spanking her on the back to get her to stop, as he had seen his mother do.

Then came a time when Mary had been punished by May for something she should not have done, and feeling rebellious afterward, the little girl went out of the house.

"Peep, peep," she heard just behind her as she walked along. A little baby chicken was following her. Mary turned around and spanked the little chick, sort of in revenge for her own punishment.

That was the end for that little chicken. Of course, Mary did not mean to kill it, and was perhaps too young to realize what she had done, but Suwano saw what happened, and she took the chicken to her mother.

Instead of spanking Mary again, May talked to her about what she had done, trying to make her understand she must not do such things, and that it was wrong to take her feelings out on the poor little chicken.

May loved her children dearly, and wanted them all to be happy, but she knew they must be trained and guided into the way of right, and for her to allow overindulgence of personal feelings or selfish desires would not help them find happiness nor the right road in life.

She taught them to be honest, obedient, and to act properly, and they were not allowed to use bad language. Also, they were not to mistreat their pets but be kind to animals.

They received a lecturing from her when she found out about the experiment they had tried on the cat. The children had heard that a cat would always land on its feet when it fell from a height, so they took the cat upstairs and dropped her out of the window while holding her feet up, for they wanted to see her turn over on the way down and land on her feet, if she would.

Another time Ernest and Lydia had tied the cat's feet and thrown her out to the dog, because the cat would always fight the dog whenever he came near her and her kittens. But the dog just looked at the cat; he wasn't interested in getting even then.

Doing such things as these was not being kind, and Mother May warned them that she would do more than just talk to them if they continued to do things like that.

Each child was given a small share of the home responsibilities as soon as they were able to handle little tasks. There was work for all of them, both indoors and out and helping take care of the younger ones. May made sure they all learned how to work as soon as they were old enough to understand and do things.

Alden had always worn a beard—May did not know what her husband would look like without one. He had always had a beard all these sixteen years since they were married. She really thought he had a rather long face and had wondered why none of their children did.

Then one day he shaved off his beard for the first time and she found out what her husband really looked like!

Baby Mary would have nothing to do with this strange new father. She would only turn her head away from him and refused to look at him until some time had passed and the strangeness had worn off. After she got used to seeing him without the beard, everything was all right again.

In the evening after he made this change in his appearance, he decided to see if anyone could be fooled as to his identity. He put on a coat that belonged to someone else, and wore a hat pulled down at a different angle than he usually wore it. Then he set out for his parent's home.

When he had knocked at the door and someone came to answer, he hesitated to speak for fear of being recognized at once, so he let them speak first.

"How do you do? Won't you come in?"

This gave him the opportunity needed, so without speaking a word, he walked in and was given a chair. It was cold out and no one wanted to hold the door open long.

But he could not long avoid speaking, so he tried to disguise his voice by using a different tone than his usual one. He was recognized at once, however, when he spoke.

"Why, it's Alden!" they exclaimed, and his disguise came to an end.

During the summer months children often became ill with what was commonly called summer complaint. Suwano seemed to have this trouble more than the others did, but it did not seem to bother Mary at all. May wondered what made the difference and thought perhaps it might be because of the different sort of things they liked to eat.

Mary would often take her little cup to the barn at milking time to get fresh warm milk in it to drink, and when Mother May skimmed the cream off the pans of milk in the milk house, Mary liked to be there with her cup and get some of the cream. She also liked to gather smartweed blossoms and eat them. May thought these habits might be helping to keep Mary in better health.

Suwano did not have a very good appetite. Sometimes she would come to the table when a meal was ready, look it over, and say that there was nothing to eat, because there was nothing there that she wanted. She was very thin, cried easily, and once became so ill that May sent Alden to get a doctor.

Knowing that her father was bringing a doctor to see her must have made Suwano feel very important, for by the time he arrived, she did not seem to be sick at all, and met him at the door.

"Are you Doctor Sloan or Doctor Street?" she asked.

"Well," the doctor remarked, "I don't think there's anything the matter with you!" And he didn't do anything for her at all.

Soon after he left, she was as sick as before, so Alden brought the other doctor out to see her. He was more understanding and helpful.

Ernest wanted very much to have a brother, so when he learned that a new baby was expected, he hoped it would be a boy. May's eighth child was born on November 20, 1887, but Ernest was disappointed to learn it was "just another girl." She was named Inez Lucinda.

Chapter 8

Plains Valley

Mary stood looking at her baby sister a long time.

"She has blue eyes with a boy's head in them," she finally remarked. Mary was seeing the reflection of her own head in baby Lou's eyes, and it looked like a boy's head to her, because her hair was cut short to save extra work for her ever-busy mother.

Inevitably someone asked Mary how she liked her new sister, but they were a bit surprised by her forthright answer.

"I don't like her," she said.

"What shall we do with her then?"

"Give her to Mrs. Adams." This would solve the problem as far as Mary was concerned, for she was jealous of the attention being given the new baby.

One cold day the children were standing with their backs to the heating stove to get warm, when their father came in from outdoors.

"I smell smoke," he said. "Guess I'd better go upstairs and see if there might be something too near the stovepipe up there."

Without stopping to remove his wraps or the heavy boots he was wearing, he went up the stairs. Suwano started to move away from the stove, and it was then that Lydia realized what it was her father had smelled.

"Wannie's on fire!" she yelled.

Down the stairs Alden came as quickly as he could in his heavy boots. And Suwano went running to meet him. They met at the bottom of the stairway, and he quickly extinguished the smoldering fire before it had time to burst into flame.

The long sash tied in a large bow in the back of her dress had been too close to the stove and had begun to smoke and turn black. This caused the odor of smoke which Alden noticed more than the others because he had just come in from the fresh air outside.

"You girls must be more careful," May told them, "and don't stand so close to the stove."

The girls, that is, Lydia and Suwano, were lots of help to May, doing little tasks so that she had more free time for larger ones. They helped take care of Mary and baby Lou when their mother was sewing or working outdoors. One evening while they were washing the dishes, Suwano, who was doing the drying, began to talk about breaking dishes, just in fun.

"Maybe I'll break some of them now," she said as she picked up the stack of saucers with two cups on them, to put them away in the cupboard.

The cups and saucers suddenly crashed to the floor and were broken into many pieces.

Alden and May were in the living room, May holding the baby on her lap.

"Go give Suwano a spanking," she said to her husband.

But he wouldn't go, so she gave the baby to him, picked up something for a paddle on the way, and gave Suwano a hard spanking. The girl did not soon forget that one. Sometimes, when she got stubborn and wasn't going to do as Mother May asked, she would be reminded.

"I'll have to get a switch, I guess," May would remark. Then Suwano would say, "I will, I will," which meant obedience, and the problem was settled again, at least temporarily.

Usually on Christmas Day the Pettegrew family got together. This family gathering was held either at Alden's home, or at his parent's home, and sometimes others of the family would come. All had a good time visiting together; there would be a big dinner, fun and gifts for the children, and perhaps a Christmas tree.

One of Mary's gifts was a big picture book. The next morning May discovered Mary sitting on the floor, busily at work cutting the pictures out of her nice new book!

This year the children heard a noise on the roof early Christmas morning, so the older ones told Mary that it was Santa Claus. There was a big Christmas tree with decorations and gifts for the children on it.

One of Mary's gifts was a big picture book. The next morning May discovered Mary sitting on the floor, busily at work cutting the pictures out of her nice new book! The cover had a very pretty picture on it, so May took that and put it up on the wall, thus salvaging that much of the book.

In 1888 May took Mary, Lou, and Ernest with her to Grand Island to visit her sister Melinda.

Ernest was twelve years old now, and able to help a great deal on the farm. He fed the hogs, and cleaned the barn after the stock went out to pasture and did other such tasks.

With Lydia helping him, he cultivated the corn. She drove the team, while he handled the cultivator. They were working in the cornfield one day when Ernest suddenly felt something run up his leg. He thought it was a lizard, so he grabbed it through his pants leg and held it so tight that when he let go, down dropped a dead mouse.

Lydia thought this was very funny to see her brother alarmed by a little mouse. When May heard about it, she was reminded of her experience with the mouse in the grain she was sacking.

Alden's sister, Lucinda, taught the Adams school that fall. One day Mary was allowed to go with the older ones to visit school. Sitting with Lydia, she was wishing for something to do when she saw her sister put her slate away. Lydia had just finished working out her arithmetic problems on the slate and put it in her desk ready to hand in to the teacher later, but of course, Mary did not understand this, and she wanted to mark on the slate.

She got the slate out of Lydia's desk, rubbed out what was on it, and began marking on the slate for something to do, like the others.

Suddenly Lydia saw what Mary had done, and she began to cry, because she knew she would have to work her problems all over again. Aunt Lou came over, and finding out what had happened, helped Mary understand why she must not erase things on the school slates.

Before school let out for the day, May came carrying baby Lou to visit school and walk home with the children.

The school children put on a program in the schoolhouse one evening and most of the families in the district attended. Lydia was dressed up in old clothes for her part in it, a recitation entitled "The Drunkard's Child." Part of her act was to cry when she reached a certain place in the sad story.

But when Lydia put her head down and began to cry, Mary thought it was for real, so she climbed down from her seat in the audience before anyone realized what she was going to do and started up the aisle toward Lydia.

"Don't ky, Lillie, don't ky," she implored sympathetically.

Lydia could hardly keep from laughing when she was supposed to be crying, and most of the audience did laugh, while May went up to get Mary, take her back to her seat and try to explain to her that Lydia was only playing at crying.

Because she had not always been allowed to attend school during her early years, May was determined that her children should secure all the education possible. She had not lost her own thirst for knowledge either, but did all the reading she had time for whenever there was something worth reading available to her.

Often, while she worked late in the evening, sewing for her family or for others, Alden would read to her as she worked. Sometimes she sewed until midnight.

Among the few books they owned was a history of the world by Gibbon and a story of missionary work in India. They also had a book on the subject of agriculture, a concordance, and of course, the Bible. May often read passages from the Bible and told Bible stories to her children.

Charles Pettegrew, Alden's younger brother, was now twenty-one years of age and ready to launch out for himself. Two of his friends, Jim and Doc Bradley, had become much interested in the Dakota Territory, planning to go there soon, and wanted Charlie to go along with them. They were going to settle on the western plains where new land, lopped off the reservations, had just been opened up for settlement.

Alden thought he would like to see the country, so he and Charlie went along with the Bradley boys, just to look it over. They were much attracted to the vast grass-covered tableland region, and found the small valley where the Bradley boys settled much to their liking.

This was the high plains region which spread all around the Black Hills, and this area had an interesting history. There the buffalo had roamed not many years before, making it the happy hunting ground of the Sioux Indians. The Dakota tribe, for whom the territory was named, had continued to hold this area because there seemed to be very little to attract the white man there. However, as soon as the buffalo were killed off, and so disappeared from the plain, cattle were driven up from Texas to replace the buffalo as a food supply for the Indians on the reservations and the soldiers stationed in the area. It was then that the white man began to realize what good grazing land this would be for raising cattle.

The Great Plains became the last stomping ground of the true American cowboy as he herded the cattle ranging around the Black Hills. But the severe winter of 1886–1887, with its heavy snows, high winds, and many blizzards, brought starvation and death to most of the great cattle herds. This gave impetus to the homesteaders.

Plains Valley was in the southwestern corner of the territory, and the Pettegrew brothers returned to eastern Nebraska full of enthusiasm for the idea of pulling up stakes and moving there too.

"We saw some wonderful country there, May," Alden told his unenthusiastic wife. "Plains Valley looked very good to me. It is a grass covered, level land, surrounded by rolling hills. I liked it fine, and I think you would like it there too."

"But why should we move away from here?" May asked. "I like it here and I don't want to even think about leaving. We have built up our homestead into a good farm now after all these years of struggle and hard work, and we have a good home here. Who can tell what we will have if we move away from all this and try to start over again in a new country?"

"I have heard the climate there is better than it is here," Alden continued, refusing to be talked out of his enthusiasm. "Perhaps we would have better health in that location then we have had here."

May talked it over with her mother-in-law.

"Here we have an orchard, with apples and some other fruit too," she began. "We have grapes, strawberries, a good garden, the maple grove, a nice house, and other good buildings. It is hard to think of going away and leaving all this."

"Yes, I know," Mother Pettegrew agreed. "I do not want to leave here, either. But my Charlie is going, and I am afraid that he might get in bad company if he goes so far away alone, with none of his family anywhere near. He is young yet, and not settled down."

May found herself outnumbered and on the losing side. She realized that she would soon be taking up her journey westward again, after more than thirty years spent in western Iowa and eastern Nebraska. It seemed hard to start making the necessary plans, but she had learned to accept what could not be changed. Before long Melissa May's scarred hands were busy with preparations to embark upon another new life experience.

Alden sold forty acres of the homestead to their nearest neighbor whose land it joined, Mr. Adams, and thus obtained the necessary money to finance the move. The remaining forty, on which the buildings, grove, and orchard stood, was rented to another family.

Farm implements and household goods were readied for the journey and taken to town where they were loaded in an emigrant railroad car. Four horses and six cows were to be shipped in the car, too, along with all the other family possessions except the personal things May and the girls would need for their journey.

It was a cold, windy day in April, 1889 when the packing was finished and the car loaded and ready to be picked up by a train going west.

Suwano stayed with her grandmother that day while Ernest and Lydia helped with the last cleanup work to be done at home. Late in the afternoon she returned home but found the house empty and no one anywhere around the homestead. It looked very lonesome there.

By evening. Alden, Ernest, and Charlie were traveling by train in the emigrant car with the family possessions on the way to Oelrichs, in Dakota Territory. Mother Pettegrew would stay with her daughter, Carrie, in North Bend, Nebraska, until a home of some sort was ready for her in Plains Valley. Dora was teaching, and so would stay until school closed, but Lucinda was going along with Father Pettegrew, May, and the children to Plains Valley. They were to leave a few days later on a passenger train which would travel faster than the freight train. This would give time for the emigrant car to reach Oelrichs first.

Alden and the boys enjoyed getting off the train and looking around at stops along the way.

"Jack seems to enjoy these stops as much or more than we do, doesn't he, Pa?" Ernest remarked, as they walked along with the dog running ahead of them.

"Yes, but you better be sure he gets back on the train when we do," was his father's comment.

The time came, however, when Jack did not board the train with them when it was ready to move on, and his absence was not noticed until after the train began to travel.

"I don't see Jack anywhere," Alden said to his son, "Didn't he get on the train?" There was a pause in the conversation after this question.

"Look, Pa!" Ernest said finally, pointing down the track from the end car where they were standing, "There he is, trying his best to catch up with us."

But Jack was too late to catch the train and was soon left far behind as the train gathered speed for the long journey ahead.

"Can't we do anything?" the boy asked.

"Well, we can't stop the train, nor go back to get him," was Alden's comment. "But we can get a new dog after we get settled in Plains Valley."

Meanwhile, back at the Adams home, May was getting the rest of the family ready to board the train. "You will travel faster than you have ever gone before," Father Pettegrew told his granddaughters. It was to be their first ride on a train, so of course, they were excited about it.

"When do we start?"

"How long will we be on the train?"

Grandfather tried to answer their questions and tell them something of what it would be like.

Some things had to be left behind, like Mary's little red wagon, which Walter Adams wanted so badly.

May had decided to let him have it because his family had been such good neighbors. They would get Mary another little red wagon in Dakota.

Mr. Adams took them all to the depot in Scribner very early in the morning, so they would be sure not to miss the train. All that day and all the following night they traveled, arriving at Oelrichs the second day, having crossed nearly the entire state of Nebraska from east to west on the main line. At Dakota Junction in northwestern Nebraska, they had changed to a branch line, the Northwestern, which had been built only two or three years before and ran through Oelrichs and on toward the Black Hills.

Alden was waiting for them with the wagons loaded and the teams hitched up and ready to go. Charlie and Ernest had already started out on horseback, driving the cattle.

"We have a long way to travel yet," Alden said when he met them at the depot. "Come and get in the wagon, girls, so we can be on our way. It's about thirty-five miles to the valley."

In the afternoon the wagons overtook the boys and the stock, so they all traveled together the rest of the way, but darkness overtook them before they reached their destination. When they stopped to rest and eat their evening meal, it seemed that they would have to camp out for the night.

"I think we had better wait until morning to go on," Alden told them. "I don't know just where we are, but we can see better when it is daylight."

The younger children were very tired and sleepy, so May put them to bed as soon as supper was over. Father Pettegrew decided to take a little walk, but after going just a short distance he saw some lights.

I may as well go over there and see what I can find out, he thought.

The lights proved to be the lanterns of a camp for the men who were working on the new B & M Railroad line. Some of the men knew the Bradley boys and where they lived, so they told him how to get to their place, which was not far away.

Father Pettegrew returned to the wagons and told Alden what he had found out.

"We had best go on tonight," Alden told the others, "for then we can have a better place to sleep."

"And we will be all ready to start work in the morning," May added as she went to wake the sleeping children. They objected to waking up so soon, but it was only a short ride, and then everyone had a place to sleep inside. Some slept on the floor in the house, and the rest slept in the barn on the hay.

They built a typical homesteader's residence on their claim, except that it was perhaps somewhat longer than most of the tar-paper-covered shacks to be seen scattered about on the plains. It was just a plain building about sixteen by thirty feet in size, banked up with sod around the outside for added protection from the wind.

Northeast of Plains Valley there was a strip of timber extending from the Black Hills, where Father Pettegrew cut logs and hauled them to the valley to build a log house for his home.

The land had not yet been surveyed, but according to "Squatter's Rights" those who settled on the land had the first right to it when it was surveyed. Other settlers came to the valley, but all were to discover before long that they could not get good water there. It was all too alkali, some more and some to a lesser degree, but some of it really horrible.

The settlers dug wells here, and they dug wells there in the valley, but not one of them produced good water. Search as they might, it seemed impossible to find any good water by digging for it. Plains Creek was fed by a spring somewhere in the hills, so its water was not as strong of alkali as the water in the wells, but the horses hooves became loosened from standing and walking in the alkali mud, and the hogs would not drink the water at all.

When the log house was ready to live in, Mother Pettegrew came from Nebraska. She tried to cook beans but found that they never would become tender in this alkali water, even though she cooked them all day long. It couldn't be used for cooking or to drink.

They built a typical homesteader's residence on their claim, except that it was perhaps somewhat longer than most of the tar-paper-covered shacks to be seen scattered about on the plains.

Dora came to the valley, too, after her school closed for the summer, and next to join them was Hattie and her family. They came about two months after Alden's family did, and Frank staked out a 160-acre claim on Cole Creek, about four miles west of the Pettegrews.

Uncle Frank had a yoke of oxen, and all the children wanted to go along the day he took Hattie to look at their land, so he hitched the oxen to a wagon, and off they all went. But he had forgotten to water the oxen, and they were very thirsty. Smelling water, away they ran with their precious cargo, straight toward an open well-hole.

Hattie screamed, and Frank did his best to stop or change the course of the thirsty beasts as they rushed on toward the well which was full of water, but his efforts availed little until they came to a pile of posts. These were directly in the path of the oxen, so they ran over them heedlessly, but this checked their speed and blocked the wagon.

When any of the family went to the nearest store for supplies, they always took barrels along in the wagon so they could bring some good water back with them when they returned. Collins was a little settlement store about twelve miles away located near the Nebraska state line. Many such little settlements had sprung up along the route of the rails as they pushed their way through the new country. Buildings in these settlements were usually tar-paper-covered shacks, too, at first, like the homesteaders built. Later Collins became a small town, and the name was changed to Ardmore.

They were all settled in their new homes before the first train came through on the new B & M Railroad line. The children all watched it go through the valley, and one of the horses saw it, too, from the field where he was grazing. He took off after it, as far as he could go in the pasture.

"Look at that horse," said Lydia, pointing to the pasture. "He wants to go back to Nebraska. The train brought him here, so maybe he thinks it will take him back."

"Well, I'd like to go back there too," Suwano remarked, and the others agreed with this.

So would I, thought May, who had overheard the children discussing the matter. She remembered how hesitant she was about leaving, and how uncertain she had been about trying to make a new start in this unknown land, but she refrained from saying anything like "I told you so," to her husband about it, for what good would that do?

Chapter 9

Jack and the Longhorns

The valley was about five and a half miles wide by eight miles long, and there was not a tree anywhere in it. Sometimes it seemed that the ground had raised up into a mountain between their house and Father Pettegrew's cabin so they couldn't see it. The two homes were about a mile apart. May told the children that this was a mirage, like the oasis sometimes seen on the desert where there is none. It was sort of a reflection, thrown onto the plain, of a mountain somewhere else.

Alden fenced his 160 acres and fenced off forty acres for a pasture. In Nebraska a forty-acre pasture had kept the cows and horses quite well fed, but he soon learned that it wouldn't keep six head here in Plains Valley, so he had to turn the cattle out onto the range. It became Ernest's job to herd them, because they would get lost among the other range cattle if not herded.

Ernest rode one of the horses to do this work, for he had to take the cattle quite a distance for water after Plains Creek dried up.

Alden had also expected to farm here as he had in Nebraska, because he had been told that one could raise most anything here that one cared to plant. However, he soon learned that the climate was too dry. There was not enough moisture in the ground, rich though the soil seemed to be, especially not this year. A great drought fell over all the central states that year.

Charlie's friends, Jim and Doc, were often at the Pettegrew home, and they liked to tease Mary.

"You are my girl, aren't you, Mary?" one of them would ask.

"No, you aren't," the other one would counter. "You're my girl."

They would ask her other questions and tell her to do things. When she got tired of their fun and would talk back to them, they were very amused. She would say, "I'm not going to do it," in answer to some of their requests and then they would laugh.

This only made her bolder with the back talk, and it did not amuse her mother.

One day May asked her little daughter to do something for her.

"I'm not going to do it," came Mary's quick response.

But this time she said it to the wrong person, if she expected to get a laugh, for she received a sound spanking for it instead. She never said those words to her mother again.

Because of the drought, most of their crops dried up before they were mature. But their worst problem was to get water for home use and for the stock to drink. When the creek began drying up, their problems grew.

They dug shallow wells in the creek bed to collect water, but finally there was so little water in these wells that they had to put a ladder down to get the water and dip it up with a cup!

A bachelor neighbor, Mr. Ingler, had started a well in the creek bed and then a rain came up during the following night. It rained just enough to make the earth around his well very muddy.

In the morning Suwano and Mary went down to watch him working, and they got into this gumbo, as the mud was called, around the well. It clung to their feet when they tried to walk, so their feet got heavier with each step they took. Mary just gave up trying.

Mr. Ingler told them to step on the mud that clung to one foot, with the other foot, which would help pull the gumbo off as they took the next step, but Mary had the answer to that idea.

"I'm not going to do it," she said, so Suwano helped her get out of the mud by doing it for her.

The Bar-T Ranch headquarters were located on Hat Creek where the Pettegrews sometimes went to get water. On these occasions the children all liked to go along so they could watch the cowboys at work while their elders filled the barrels with water.

During the seventies, after gold was discovered by the whites in the Black Hills, the Indians were put on reservations and not too kindly treated by some of the white folks. Nearest to the valley was the Pine Ridge Reservation.

At this time there was still a great deal of unrest among the Indians of the area, and the settlers often had reason to fear trouble. Bands of Indians sometimes left the reservation, usually to go hunting. Then scouts were sent out to find how many had gone, where they were, and what they were doing.

Scouts sometimes passed through Plains Valley and stopped at the Pettegrew home. Frontier hospitality always prevailed in May's home, and this continued to be true all down through the years.

And, of course, Indians often stopped at the homes in the valley to beg. Sometimes the children would hear the sound of approaching horses while they were busy playing outside, and looking up, they would see a lot of Indians.

On one such occasion they looked up and saw two Indians riding at a gallop toward the house. Dinner was just over when these two arrived, but of course they wanted something to eat, and expected to be fed.

The Indians sat down at the dinner table which had not yet been cleared. A bowl containing just a little applesauce was sitting on the table, so they reached over and sampled it with their fingers. After finishing what was left in the bowl, they made motions with their hands to catch May's attention and tell her by gestures that they wanted her to put more applesauce into the bowl. But she did not have any more of it, so they had to be satisfied with something else.

During that summer in Plains Valley, the Pettegrews took time out from their labors for a pleasure excursion. Leaving Ernest and Lydia at home to take care of things there, Alden and May took the younger ones and went with Charlie, Lou, Dora, and the Bradley boys on a trip. They took two wagons and were away from home for several days, camping out overnight first at Cascade. From there they went to Hot Springs and camped beside the warm water there.

This town has grown up around the thermal springs located there, hence the name, Hot Springs. Located at the southern edge of the Black Hills, along Fall River, it had become a health and pleasure resort because of the warm mineral water. The town itself was merely one long street right along the river, with some of the dwellings of the residential section built on the hillside. These homes were reached by stairs built up the slope from the business district below.

The Indians had long before brought their sick to bathe in the waters. Legend tells that a battle for possession of this area had ended in an agreement among the tribes to regard the location as neutral ground. Now the spring waters were widely advertised as a cure for many ills. Little Fall River, fed by the springs, never changes temperature, and the climate of the vicinity seems to remain warmer than the surrounding area.

Back home from their trip, they felt a little better acquainted with the Dakota Territory.

Scattered about among the sagebrush in the slate hills were some wild plum trees, or bushes, and although they did not have many plums on them this year, fruit of any kind was worth looking for; they had so little of it. While the family was picking wild plums one day, their little dog encountered a rattlesnake and quickly killed it.

Immediately another rattler appeared, presumably the mate of the first one. The little dog tackled this one, too, but the snake was too quick for him and struck the dog on his tongue. He kept at his task and killed this rattler also, biting it in two and flinging it away. But soon the deadly venom did its work. Dog and snake both lost their lives in what was truly a deadly combat.

There were also some sandberries in the hills, prickly pear cactus, and currants in the vicinity, and choke cherries grew in some places along the small streams.

May learned that it was best to glance often at the sky, and she learned to tell from its appearance when a storm was coming. She taught the children this habit also, so they might be able to reach shelter before a storm could catch them unprotected on the prairie. If any of the family, especially the children, were out in the open away from home when she noticed signs of a sudden storm coming up May was very uneasy and watchful for their return.

On one such occasion Ernest was out on the horse with the cattle. He saw that a storm was coming, so he hurried toward home as fast as he could. The rest of the family were all inside the house hoping that he would make it home in time. He rode as fast as the horse would take him, right toward the house, and those watching from inside opened the door as he came near. He jumped off the horse and ran in the door just as the storm broke.

It was a hailstorm, and Alden held the horse at the door so the hail would not strike its head. But this horse, whose name was Selim, did not like to remain mostly outside with only his head in, so he came right in the house. After all, why should he stay outside when shelter was right there—good horse sense to come on in!

The hail made such a noise as it struck the roof that the family could scarcely hear one another speaking, even when they talked as loud as they could.

Sometimes a white bulldog would come to visit, and often would make himself at home with the Pettegrews when his owner, Mr. Ingler, was away. This dog was in the yard when May noticed that a stray pig had wandered into her yard. She went out to chase the pig away, thinking she would enlist the dog's aid.

"Sic 'em," she said to the white dog. He ran after the pig and caught it by the side of the neck. He would not let go, and May could not get him to let go.

Alden's sister, Lou, was in the house, so she came out to help May, who had by then found a stick to use on the dog. Between them they finally got the dog and pig separated.

"I don't think we want that kind of dog around here," May said after she told Alden about the experience. "But I do think that we need to have a dog to help with herding the cattle."

"Yes," he agreed, "we'll have to get another dog."

Not long after this Frank stopped by on his way home from a trip to Oelrichs.

"Hello!" he called from outside. "Is anyone at home?"

May went out to see what he wanted.

"Where is Ernest? Is he somewhere around?"

"I think he's coming," she replied. "What do you have there, Frank?"

"Well, as you can see, I have a couple of half-grown English Shepherd dogs. I was wondering if you folks would like to have one of them, since you don't have a dog now."

"Where did you get them?" one of the children asked, as they gathered around their uncle's wagon to look at the dogs.

"I saw them at the stables in Oelrichs," he answered. "Someone had left them there, so I was told. Their former owner was headed for Wyoming when he stopped there, and intended to take the dogs along with him to use as sheep dogs. But they were forgotten. Since then the children around the place have teased and tormented the pups, though, and they have become quite cross."

By this time Ernest had arrived at the wagon, too, and saw the dogs.

"How would you like to have one of these dogs, Ernest? Come take a good look at them, and tell me which one you would like to keep."

It didn't take Ernest long to decide, because one of the pups was black with white markings, resembling the dog he had lost as they were traveling from eastern Nebraska to the Dakota Territory.

"This is the one I would like to have," he told his uncle, indicating his choice, "and I'll name him Jack too."

Jack proved to be a more savage dog than his brother, whom Uncle Frank kept for a family pet, but he was a good dog and became very loyal to his owners.

Having to spend a lot of his time herding the cattle, Ernest was glad to have the dog with him for company and help. He soon taught Jack how to help keep the cattle moving, to help him drive them to water, and help keep them separated from the wild range cattle.

Jack was very cross with strangers, especially boys. Perhaps this was because of the teasing he and his brother had received at the hands of boys while staying in the livery barn at Oelrichs. He didn't like to be petted either, which may have been the way the boys had coaxed him to be still while they tied tin cans to his tail or did other mean things.

A couple of boys came riding up to the house on their ponies one day when Alden and May were not at home. They came to buy some of May's good butter, for she made butter to sell whenever she could, just as she had in Nebraska.

While the boys were there, they offered to let Lydia and Suwano take a ride on their ponies.

The girls laid a chair across the doorway, leaving Mary and baby Lou inside the house so they couldn't come out to get in the way. Then Jack promptly sat down in front of the door to stay on guard while Lydia and Suwano were away. He wouldn't let the boys come near.

"Ernest, you better herd the cattle over near Cole Creek today," Alden told his son at the breakfast table.

"How would you like to go along with Ernest and spend the day with your cousins?" May asked the girls.

"Oh, yes, that would be fun," they agreed.

"Then get busy with the dishes," she told them. "You can be finished by the time Ernest is ready to go."

Aunt Hattie's children were Ethel, between Lydia and Suwano in age; Charlie, next younger; George, a bit older than Mary; and a baby younger than Lou, named Mamie. Their home was near Cole Creek where the cattle had to be taken for water since Plains Creek had dried up.

Of course, Ernest took Jack along to help with the herding.

They had around twenty-five head of cattle altogether, with quite a number of young included in this count. By this time Jack had learned how to be a lot of help; in fact, he could do most of the work for Ernest, and he cooperated well with the horse in handling the cattle.

As usual, Ernest rode a horse, but the girls had to walk.

Jack's brother, Fido, was there to welcome them when they arrived, and the two dogs seemed to have a good time together while the children were playing. Fido brought Jack a bone, and they did not fight over the food when they were fed.

Ernest had to keep the cattle in sight, so while they all played together most of the time, he often stopped to check on where his charges were, and sometimes sent Jack to bring them back because they had begun to wander away. Most of the day was spent in this manner, until Ernest knew it was time for the cattle to be started toward home.

He started out walking with the girls and leading the horse, while Jack went ahead to drive the cattle. But along the way a large herd of range cattle was sighted ahead, so he sent Jack to drive them out of the way so the two herds would not get together and mix.

While the dog was doing this, two longhorn steers suddenly appeared, coming from across the railroad tracks close by, and joined the children's herd of cattle.

Ernest took an empty cartridge out of his pocket and blew into it to make a shrill whistle—the call for Jack to return. He came promptly, and was sent to drive the steers away, but this was not easy.

The dog would get the two longhorns on the run and headed away from his herd, but they were fast runners, and could outrun the dog. They kept right on running, not away, but in a circle which led them around and right back where they could join the herd before the dog could get back to head them off. So Ernest had to get on his horse and help the dog.

They finally managed to get the steers separated from the cattle just before they arrived at the home corral. But again, the longhorns circled around and came back. This time they jumped the fence into the north pasture.

Jack was all tired out, so he had gone to his allotted place to rest while Alden and Ernest were doing the milking and other evening chores. But after supper was over, they called the dog to come along with them to the north pasture.

It was dark by this time, so they could not see the strays, but they told Jack to take those steers out of the field, and away he went. He knew where they were, or soon found them, and then they went over the fence, just as they had come in. Ernest and his father heard the wires ting, that was how they knew Jack had accomplished exactly what they had sent him to do.

Yes, indeed, a good dog was a lot of help on the range, and around the farm too. Jack was becoming much more than just a herd dog. He was a friend and protector of the children, and the guardian of everything on the claim.

Alden finally admitted it was time to give up. There just was not any use trying to make a place for themselves in Plains Valley under such adverse circumstances.

"It's hopeless," he told May, despondently. "There is no future for us here; no hope that we can get enough water for the stock and crops. The

> *While the dog was doing this, two longhorn steers suddenly appeared, coming from across the railroad tracks close by, and joined the children's herd of cattle.*

only thing for us to do is to move away. We must find a better place and start over again."

"I'll be glad enough to leave here," May agreed. "But couldn't we go back to our homestead in Nebraska? That is what I would like to do, and I know the children would like that too." She was thinking wistfully of the pleasant home they had left behind them to come to Plains Valley.

But Alden slowly shook his head.

"No, we can't do that. We can't because there isn't enough land left. You know, we sold part of the place, and what we have left is not enough for us to make a living on. We will have to find something better than this here in this area if we can."

It was about six months after their arrival in Plains Valley when Alden set out to look for a new location. Some families had already left the valley, and most of the remaining residents were planning to go.

Chapter 10

Another Move

About twelve miles southwest of Oelrichs, and only four miles north of the Nebraska state line, Alden located some land that he liked and which he had reason to believe would be better than in the valley.

He had already used up most of his homestead rights in Nebraska, so he could not hope to get enough land for their needs in this way again. However, there was the "right of preemption," established by Congress in 1841, under which he could obtain land. He filed an application for a preemption claim of 160 acres.

According to the law, filing on such a claim gave him preference ahead of all others in buying the land after living on it and making improvements over a six-month period of time. Then he could buy it from the government for $1.25 an acre and receive a clear title.

The preemption right was established to prevent claim jumping, and it was abolished about two years after this.

The total loss of their crops that season left most of the new settlers without supplies for the winter and also without seed for planting next spring, because they had not had time to build up a surplus. For these reasons some of the settlers were giving up and returning east.

The Indians as well as the whites were affected by the drought, although the red man didn't do much farming. It added to the dissatisfaction already felt among them because of their loss of the buffalo and their land, and the failure of the government's new Indian Agents in fulfilling treaty agreements about supplies which the Indians needed. Government provisions intended for them were often disposed of in ways more profitable to those agents.

A Nevada Paiute Indian claimed to have had a vision of a Messiah who would restore the buffalo to the plains and make the white men disappear. Representatives from the Cheyenne and Sioux Indians on the reservations joined with others in a large gathering in Nevada where they were instructed in the new "religion" which had been developed from this vision, and which became known as the Messiah Craze.

Warfare did not seem to be a part of it, but the Ghost Dance connected with it became a means of expressing pent-up emotions against the whites. As talk of serious Indian trouble began spreading among the settlers, some became alarmed, but Alden and May were not much concerned about this situation. They had the more immediate problem of moving to a new location.

They moved out of their tar-paper-covered "long house" into a smaller building, so the house could be taken apart. Then the lumber was hauled across the prairie on wagons to the new location where it was to be rebuilt into a house again.

Most of a day was required to make the one-way trip with a load, for it was thirty-five miles. A neighbor near their new claim, Mr. Nelson, helped with the moving.

As soon as the long house was put up, and one room enclosed, or finished up so it could be lived in, May took the younger children and moved in, leaving Ernest and Lydia in the valley to take care of the stock.

Everything movable was taken from their valley location and moved to the new home site during the fall and early winter months. Providentially, for them, it was not a stormy winter. The weather remained mild with no high winds or heavy snowstorms to interrupt their work.

During this time of transition, the Dakotas became states, along with Montana and Washington. They were no longer in the Dakota Territory but were living in the state of South Dakota now.

While the menfolks were all gone on one of their trips back to the valley, a near neighbor came over early one morning, before daylight.

"Mrs. Pettegrew, I think the Indians are coming," he said to May when she opened the door. "We've been hearing them yelling over toward where the German folks live, so I thought I ought to warn you. Perhaps you and the children better come up to our place."

Mary and Lou were still in bed, but Suwano was up, and she went outside with May to listen, but all they could hear was the howling of coyotes.

"That doesn't sound anything like Indians to me," May remarked, undisturbed. "Anyway, I think we are safe enough right here. Thank you just the same," she told him, and went back to her work.

Coyotes often howled in the night and early morning, so May did not become alarmed. She thought perhaps Mr. Poole just wanted to see if he could scare them as a joke.

The unfinished half of their house was used as a shelter for the team at night, and the chickens were kept in one end of it. Although the weather did not get stormy, it turned really cold, so sometimes the eggs were frozen when they brought them in the house. During the coldest nights the hens could be heard making a noise—a sort of slow, drawn out *caw, caw, caw,* because of the cold, and sometimes in the morning, after such a night, a hen would be found frozen. They lost a number of the chickens in this manner.

Charlie went to work as a freighter that winter like many other young men did about that time. While away on one of his trips he bought an Indian pony and had another fellow take it to Alden's place for him as he had to go on another trip, so did not have time to do it himself.

Suwano was the only one at home when the pony arrived, so she had a nice surprise for the others when they returned home. Of course, the children were all excited about the pony and wished very much that they might have one for their own use.

As soon as possible a corral was built for the livestock, and then all the cattle were brought over from the valley, so Ernest and Lydia did not have to stay over there anymore. The barn and chicken house had been reconstructed before there was time to finish the house, but in time they had two rooms once again.

The children liked to play in the attic above the two rooms, but at first only Ernest slept up there because Alden had not had time to put a ladder up. Later the attic became their bedroom, and Ernest slept below. They all had hay or straw stuffed into ticks for mattresses on their beds.

Alden's father filed on a preemption claim in this locality also, and his log house had to be taken down, moved, and rebuilt again. They also filed on timber claims of 160 acres. In order to secure title to this land they were to plant ten acres of trees on the claim.

Charlie, Dora, and Lou took homesteads soon after they came over to the area. All three of these claims were nearby.

Oelrichs, the nearest town, was large enough to boast of a bank, a post office, church, hotel, restaurant, a couple of stores, a lumberyard, and enough people that a two-room school was necessary. There was also a depot, and the stables where Frank had found the two dogs.

Horsehead Creek was only a mile east of the Pettegrew's home. From a slope just north of the house the Black Hills could be seen, appearing as dark mountains silhouetted against the sky, more than forty miles away.

A dance was held in a nearby home not long after the newcomers were settled, which was attended by the young folks over a wide area. May allowed her children to go and watch the dancing for a while, so they saw people from the surrounding neighborhoods for the first time. It was a treat for the younger children, for they seldom had the opportunity to go anywhere away from home.

They were soon to get away from home every weekday, however, for there was a little log schoolhouse in the community.

"I'm glad there's a school here for the children to attend," was May's comment. "Even though it only has two short terms each year, that is much better than no school at all."

> *The cart was tipped over, and Dora was thrown out. Her feet got caught in the lines as she fell out, and the horse started going around and around in a circle.*

The Prairie Flower School was less than a mile away, so when the spring term began the first of March, all three of the older ones started attending. This was the first opportunity they had to attend school since coming to Dakota, for there had been no school in Plains Valley. The two short terms of three months each were divided by a vacation in winter, as well as one in the summertime. During the winter months when the weather was often too severe for children to venture far from home alone, the school was not open. Dangerous storms often came up very suddenly on the prairie, so this was a precaution which perhaps saved the lives of many children.

Aunt Lou taught this school, where there were twenty-four students, while Dora taught the Shell school in a nearby community about four miles away. The two teachers stayed at home with their parents and drove one of their father's horses to and from their work. Dora usually drove and took Lou to her school, then went on to her own.

Driving the pony hitched to a cart, Dora stopped to visit Alden and May one evening on her way home from school. She was alone and did not stop very long. After she started toward home, a strap broke on the harness as she was driving down the lane, and the horse was unable to hold the cart back, so they began going faster and faster as the cart pushed the horse along.

One of Alden's cows was lying down in the lane and could not get up and out of the way in time, so one of the cart wheels went over her—that is, it started over, but the cow had begun getting up then. The cart was tipped over, and Dora was thrown out. Her feet got caught in the lines as she fell out, and the horse started going around and around in a circle.

Ernest was bringing the cows in for the evening milking, and saw the accident, so he ran to catch the horse to stop its circling. Alden also saw what had happened and came running to the scene. He found that his sister was stunned and was talking foolish and did not know what had happened or what she was doing. However, she was not seriously hurt, and was soon acting normal again.

Among those attending the Prairie Flower School were the Nelson girls, whose father had helped with the moving, and youths from the Mathwig, Evans, Wilkinson, and two Neff families. Young folks of all ages and sizes were in attendance, because some had not been able to attend regularly, and so were larger and older. Lola Neff was taller than the teacher, but said she was only eleven years old.

Alden had fenced a forty-acre pasture for his cattle, so they would not need to be herded, but like in Plains Valley, they soon had to be let out on the prairie where there was lots of good grass for them. This time Suwano was chosen for the job of herding, so she did not get to attend school very long. She was the youngest one of the family attending school, so it was thought she could more easily get schooling later, while it was necessary for the older ones to attend now.

She had to walk, but she had Jack to help her, and he could do most of the work for her. He seemed to know the names of all the cattle. She would tell him which one she wanted him to separate from the rest of the herd, and he would promptly bring that one out for her.

She also taught him to drive the cattle alone, with her directing him from a distance by waving her hand in the direction she wanted him to drive them. He would stop often and look back to her for more directions.

After the close of the school term, Lydia sometimes went with Suwano and Jack herding the cattle, but Alden had more important work for Ernest to do. The boy was fourteen years old now and able to do many things along with his father in the fields.

Ernest was somewhat resentful about being the only boy, oldest in a family of "just girls." However, he was fond of his five-year-old sister, Mary. Sometimes he gave her attention in the evening after the chores were finished. He would take her in her little red wagon, pulling it around and around in a circle to see how long she could stay in it, and how long he could keep the wagon from tipping over and spilling her out.

Mary, of course, thought this was great fun, and when she fell out, she would get up and get right back into the wagon again, ready for more.

May had two hens with little chickens, each in her own separate little coop that spring. Suwano claimed that one was hers, and Mary claimed the other. One evening Mary thought of giving her hen some salt, so she got some which she took out and fed to the mother hen. As a result, that hen died and left her brood of chickens without a mother. But Suwano's hen was a good mother and took all the chicks to care for as her own.

Of course, the girls knew they did not really have these hens and chicks for their very own, but Suwano did want very much to have something alive which would belong to her only.

Later she was out with May where a hen was sitting on a nest of eggs. They found that the eggs were hatching, but May knew that not all of them were good. Some were spoiled or rotten, so she started throwing those eggs away.

Suwano was watching her mother, and suddenly she thought that she heard some peeping in one of the eggs that her mother threw a long way off, so she went down to where the egg had landed and got it.

She held the egg up to her ear, and sure enough, it had a little chick in it which wasn't quite ready to pick its way out of the shell. She took it back to where May was, at the nest.

> *One day, as the chicken grew older, she was dismayed to hear it trying to crow, and before long they all knew that Biddy was not a biddy at all, but a rooster.*

"Ma, can I have this egg?" she asked, hopefully. "I think there is a live chicken in it."

"Why, yes, I guess you can have it," May answered, knowing how badly Suwano had been wanting to have something like that for her very own.

So Suwano took the egg to the house, wrapped it up to keep it warm, and began her vigil of watching and waiting for the chicken to come out.

Finally, after what seemed like a long time to her, the chick began to pick a hole in the shell, and soon it was out. Suwano thought this was the most wonderful thing in the world right then. She decided that she would call her chicken Biddy.

The little chick soon became a very special pet, to Suwano at least, and she took very good care of it. She was often seen carrying the chicken around everywhere she went, and before long it learned to follow her.

Everyone who came to the house had to hear all about Biddy, for Suwano always saw to it that they were told.

One day, as the chicken grew older, she was dismayed to hear it trying to crow, and before long they all knew that Biddy was not a biddy at all, but a rooster. That did not dampen Suwano's devotion to her pet, however, and she continued to call him Biddy just the same as before.

May grew very tired of the way this daughter of hers talked so much about that chicken to everyone who came to call, so she decided that she would put a stop to it. Charlie was the next visitor who appeared at the house after this decision, so when Suwano began talking to him, telling him all about the latest accomplishments of her chicken, May interrupted her.

"Now, Suwano," she said, "you have talked enough about him. Don't you ever say Biddy again!"

For a while the girl was quiet, but suddenly they heard a rooster crow.

"There!" she exclaimed, triumphantly, "Biddy crowed!"

Forgotten for the moment in her pride of ownership were those warning words from her mother. Then she noticed that May was looking straight at her with a very stern expression on her face, and she realized what she had done. Then she was afraid of being punished, but May had not taken it that seriously. However, after that experience, Suwano tried to keep quiet more, though she still thought as much as ever of "that chicken."

Wheat grass and buffalo grass grew all over the plains where the Pettegrews lived. When there was enough rain in the spring and early summer, there would be plenty of wheat grass to mow for hay. Alden would store a good supply of it then for the cattle's winter feed.

The buffalo grass did not grow very tall. It was a short, curly grass, and rich feed for the stock, but when the weather became hot and dry, it died down until the next spring.

During mild winters such as the last one, cattle could run out most all winter. The grass had matured, and was dry, like hay, out on the prairie, so the cattle could live on it through the winter. But when deep snows covered the prairie grass, or when it had been a dry season so the grass dried up before it matured, then the cattle had to be fed. Sometimes people would cut Russian thistles while they were young and tender, to use as a substitute for hay. The cattle liked them, but they were not good for the stock. Cows that were fed on thistles in the winter would lose their calves; either they were born dead or died a few days after birth.

The prairie soil seemed to be good, but the problem was lack of moisture. It didn't rain enough, nor was there water for irrigation on a large scale.

Alden was beginning to learn more about this country, but it would take a few more years for him to find out what it was really like and what could best be raised on the land. It certainly was not good farming country like where he had been in Nebraska. He tried raising corn on the forty acres across the road, but in later years he changed to wheat.

When there was no hail, wheat did fine if planted in the fall—and if it didn't blow out. Those who lived near a creek that did not go dry in the summer could dig a big pond in it, build a dam below this, and thus collect water for a limited amount of irrigation.

The water was much better here than in the valley. They were able to get good water for the livestock from the first, but it was not until the fourth well was dug that they found really good water for home use. This well was in the pasture across the road, which meant that water had to be carried, or hauled, from there to the house.

Alden dug a cave not far from the house as a place for May to use for butter and milk during the warm weather and for storing vegetables during the winter. He dug a hole about ten by twelve and perhaps six feet deep, then built a roof over it by using a pole for the center and putting boards up to it from each side. This was covered with sod, and a sloping door was made for the entrance at one end, with steps inside leading down to the dirt floor. This door became a fine slide for Mary and Lou to play on.

They still had to haul wood for their fuel from the timber where Father Pettegrew had gotten the logs to build his house. It was thirty or thirty-five miles to that strip of timber which extended from the Black Hills down between Hat Creek and Edgemont, so they could not make a quick trip there and back but had to camp out while felling trees and cutting them up so the wood could be loaded onto their wagons.

After May and her brothers were separated, she had lost contact with them and did not know where they were now, although she had been in touch with her sisters. But during the summer of 1890 she received a letter from Selby who had somehow found out where she was living.

He wrote her that he had continued to live with and work for the farmer where he had gone to stay after their father's death, and when he was nineteen, he married the farmer's daughter, Mary, who was then fourteen years old. They continued living with her parents for a while, then later moved on to a nearby farm.

Their first child, Coral, was born in 1871, so now May knew that Selby had a daughter older than any of her children. Coral was now married to Jim Smith—the once little boy, Jimmy, whom May had helped take care of when she was a girl.

May learned that Selby had a son, Roland, who was a little older than Ernest, a daughter, Pearl, about Suwano's age, and two younger sons, Charlie, near Mary's age, and Perry.

Selby's letter informed her that he was planning to visit her soon. He wanted to see what the Dakota country was like and thought perhaps he might come there to live. A friend, Mr. Daley, would make the trip with him.

May wondered if she would recognize her brother, for they were still not grown up when they parted, and he might have changed a lot. In fact, she had been told that Selby had grown to be quite a tall man, so she got the idea that he would be taller than his friend.

Selby Barnes and his friend got off the train three miles east of the Pettegrew claim, and walked across country to look some of it over as they came. Of course, May was expecting them, but when the two men arrived at her door, they insisted that she guess which one of them was her brother. Because of what she had heard about Selby's height, she picked the taller one, but she was wrong, for Mr. Daley was taller than her brother.

It was early when the men arrived. Lydia and Suwano were still in bed up in the attic, but they looked down to see who was there when they heard voices below, and then hurried to get dressed so they could meet their uncle.

"You know, May," Selby said, after he had seen all of her family, "I can see your children resemble mine a great deal. Mary looks like my son, Charlie, and Suwano looks some like my daughter, Pearl."

Chapter 11

Suwano's Enterprise—Selby's Story

Selby and May had much to tell each other about their experiences through the years since they had last been together.

"After Orvin, our third child, was born, we moved to Kansas," he said. But Orvin died when he was eighteen months old.

"The Santa Fe Company was building a railroad there, and I took a contract with them for boarding forty-five men at fifteen cents per meal each. While waiting for the company to get ready to lay iron, I moved lumber. The roads were good and I had a good mule team, so hauled 2,000 feet at a time.

"Then I took a contract to distribute ties for the railroad to lay the iron on, and at one time I had twenty-five teams hired, so with mine, it made twenty-six we were using. This road extended from Burlingame to Great Bend. Then we moved back to Burlingame and laid ties from there to the Arkansas River.

"After that I had a farm for six years, where I raised corn and sold it to the owner of the land for fifteen cents per bushel, delivered into his feed yard. He furnished the seed and I did the work.

"Coral married in 1887 and went with her husband to live in Missouri, and we moved to Greeley County, Nebraska, where we are now. Our stepbrother, Tom Place, lives there and we have been working together, farming and breaking in new prairie lands for others. We broke 250 acres for one man.

"Recently Jim and Coral came from Missouri to be with us, so we are all together again."

Selby went to a nearby town one day and returned with a dollars' worth of candy for May's children. This was more than they had ever had before, and more than the younger ones had even seen.

Before returning to Nebraska, he filed claim on a homestead about a mile and a half southeast of his sister's home. He would bring his family up from Nebraska before winter, he said, so May's children were looking forward to getting acquainted with the cousins.

Suwano was out with her father one evening looking at a new calf—the last arrival of the season—when she got an idea. Since she had done so well with her chicken, she decided that she would like to have that calf for her very own to raise and take care of and watch grow as she had done with the chicken. Hoping that her father might sell this calf to her, she began leading the conversation in that direction.

"How much is that calf worth, I wonder," she said half questioningly, trying not to sound too anxious. She had a little money of her own and was willing to spend it to get this calf.

"Well, I suppose about fifty cents," Alden answered.

"I'll give you fifty cents for it," she offered quickly.

"All right, you can have it."

Suwano's brown eyes shone with pleasure as she told May about this transaction, for now she was launched on a real experience in animal husbandry.

This was another dry summer. Crops dried up, and there was not any surplus of food for man or animals.

"Have you thought of a name for her yet?" her mother asked.

"Oh, yes, I'm going to call her Emmy. And I'm going to fix a special place for her."

Before long they were telling her, "You're spoiling that calf just like you did the chicken." But she didn't care if they did think so, for she was enjoying the work of taking care of Emmy.

This was another dry summer. Crops dried up, and there was not any surplus of food for man or animals. Many settlers left western South Dakota then, not only because of this second dry year in a row, but also because there were many rumors of Indian uprisings. People became alarmed, fearing that the red man would go on the warpath again.

The Pettegrews did not seem to have any fears in this regard, nor did they think of returning to the east.

Father Pettegrew and Charlie built cabins, or "homestead shacks," on Charlie's and Dora's homesteads during that summer so they could live on the land part of the time. Five years residence was required before the homesteaders could prove up and secure title to the land.

Mr. Evans came along the road driving a bunch of range cattle as Suwano was out near the road with Jack. The cattle had come in from the western range and were getting into his crops, so he was trying to drive them back where they belonged.

"Do you have a good dog there?" he asked when he saw Suwano and the dog standing there watching.

"Yes, we certainly do," she answered proudly. Jack seemed to understand every word that was said, but when Mr. Evans called to him and tried to get him to drive the cattle, Jack just stood right where he was, waiting to hear what Suwano would say next. He looked up at her but did not move.

"All right, Jack," she said finally. "You go drive those cattle away."

He took off after them as soon as she spoke, driving them just as fast as he could make them go, away and out of sight over a hill more than a half mile away.

"Say, you really do have a good dog," Mr. Evans commented, admiringly, after watching Jack perform.

On the ninth of September all the children, except Lou, were sent over to stay with their Aunt Dora in her "shanty on the claim." It was early evening when they went, and they had a good time playing games until they were tired and sleepy. Then they made beds on the floor and all slept there that night.

The next morning they arrived back home just as their father and little sister were at the breakfast table. From her high chair beside her father, Lou called to them as they entered the house.

"I got a baby! I got a baby!" she announced excitedly.

Sure enough, there was a new baby in the house—another sister. And again May chose a family name for the child, Caroline Roberts. But Mary, like Thomas of old, was the doubting one. She went to the bedroom door and looked in on her mother.

"Come on in and see your new baby sister," May called to her. Reluctantly Mary went over and stood beside the bed.

"It isn't yours," was her matter-of-fact comment, after looking at the baby for a while.

"Then who do you think she belongs to?" May asked curiously, a little amused at her daughter's attitude.

"To Mrs. Manny!" was Mary's prompt answer.

Mrs. Manny was the lady taking care of May and the new baby. But Mary soon had to accept the fact that Carrie really did belong in the family.

So many families had moved away, there were not enough students to have a school in the district that year. Dora was to teach school in Oelrichs, so she rented a house there in which to stay during the school term, which ran straight through the winter. She wanted Alden and May to let Lydia stay with her and attend school, so they decided to let her go. This meant that Suwano would be May's only helper at home.

Discovering one day that there was no water at the house and no one at home to get some for her, May had Suwano help her get a horse harnessed and hitched to a sled, and off she went with an empty barrel to get water, leaving Suwano in charge at the house.

As she was returning with the water, she noticed the barrel was sliding nearer and nearer the edge of the sled and would fall off before she could get home if something wasn't done to prevent that from happening, so without thinking of herself, she stopped and pushed the heavy barrel back where it belonged. This exertion was too much for her so soon after the birth of the baby and back to bed she had to go.

Suwano became the mainstay of the home for a time, doing most of the cooking, the housework, and taking care of the baby. But May was up and around again as soon as she could be, supervising and helping. She moved about the house by using a chair for a crutch on which to rest her bad leg and was still getting around in this manner when her brother Selby arrived, bringing his family from Nebraska.

May's children had looked forward to the coming of their uncle and aunt, with the cousins about whom they had heard so much. They knew also that Cousin Coral had two small children, Elva and Bella.

With Lydia away in Oelrichs, May's family numbered one less, but there were ten altogether in Selby's family, so that brought the total up to seventeen.

Selby had the habit of using lots of slang and swear words in his conversation. Most all of these words were new and strange to May's children, for very little such language was ever used in their hearing. But little Elvie Smith was quite used to her grandfather's strong language and often used it herself. While playing with Mary and Lou, Elvie used one of those words every time she kicked a tin can in a game they were playing together.

Lou seemed to think that this must be part of the game, or anyway a good way to play it, so she decided to adopt Elvie's method, and began repeating the same word that Elvie used every time she kicked the tin can.

When May found out what her little girl was doing, she soon put an end to it. She took Lou aside and explained that the word was not a good one to use and told her that she must not use it anymore.

Ernest and Roland drove to Oelrichs and brought Lydia home for the weekend so that she, too, could get acquainted with the cousins from Nebraska.

Now that there were others to do the work in the house, it was not so necessary for Suwano to help, so she spent more time herding the cattle again. Sometimes Cousin Pearl went along with her, but it was not long before Selby and his son-in-law had their families settled elsewhere.

Work was scarce in this area, so they went into the Black Hills area where there were sawmills, and there they got work for the winter months. Both Selby and Jim Smith were soon engaged in hauling lumber.

The hills are sometimes called an island range in the sea of the Great Plains, for they are an assembly of mountains entirely apart from the Rocky Mountains. Mining and lumber were being carried on quite extensively in the hills at that time, while herds of cattle still grazed on the lower hills and surrounding plains.

The Black Hills had been so named by the Sioux Indians because the pine forests covering the hills made them look black from a distance. An Indian legend had it that evil spirits had caused these mountains to vomit fire and stones many years before, and the volcanic peaks in the area bear out the story that there must have been volcanic action there at some time in the distant past.

This country became a part of the United States through the Louisiana Purchase, of course, but the land still belonged to the Indians really, so it was bought again, by treaty, from them. But these twice-bought hills were worth much more than their total cost, not only in yellow gold, but other minerals, and the black forests were a wealth of "green gold."

Selby and Jim hauled thousands of feet of lumber to be used in building the Evans Hotel in Hot Springs, and they hauled lumber other places as well.

It was a dark night and the lights had all been put out, for everyone in the long house had gone to bed. But Lou was crying about something instead of going to sleep like she should.

Charlie had been working for Alden lately and was staying that night with Ernest. Thinking to frighten Lou into being quiet, and hearing a cricket now and then when her voice did not drown him out, he called to her.

"You listen there," he said. "Listen! Can't you hear that cricket? You better look out or that cricket will be getting you!"

But instead of frightening her into silence, Charlie's bright idea had the opposite effect and Lou only squalled more and louder, because she was afraid the cricket might bite her or something.

Lou was easily excited, frightened, and otherwise upset and Charlie thought it fun to tease her, not only in ways like this, but he also teased her about being so fat. She was more chubby than the other children.

One time a guest arrived after the family had eaten dinner, so May prepared a meal for him in her usual hospitable manner. Seeing food being put on the table again, Lou came to the table and climbed into her chair, expecting to eat again. In contrast to Suwano, who was not much interested in food and had little appetite for it, Lou was always ready to eat.

The name "Charlie" was very much used on both sides of the family tree. Selby had a son Charlie, Hattie had a son Charlie, and there was Alden's brother Charlie. Mother Pettegrew's brother also had a son named Charlie. This was Charlie Shaw, and he lived in Missouri but came now to South Dakota for a visit. He stayed for a while with Charlie Pettegrew on his homestead.

There were lots of coyotes in the area, but Cousin Charlie had never heard them howling as they often did during the night—not before he came to South Dakota. So one night when the coyotes were doing a lot of howling, it woke him up. He jumped out of bed, grabbed his gun, and woke up his cousin.

"Get up quick!" he said with excitement. "There's something wrong at Alden's. I hear the children screaming!"

But the other Charlie just laughed and told him that it was only the coyotes howling.

If someone forgot to close and fasten the door to the chicken house in the evening, they were likely to find fewer chickens in it the next morning, for the coyotes would get them. Even in the daytime they might get them sometimes if the chickens wandered too far from home. Occasionally coyotes would get little calves and colts too.

Charlie Shaw had brought a hunting dog with him, as he liked to hunt. Sometimes Ernest went hunting for sage hens, ducks, snipe, or rabbits. There were other small animals in the area too, such as skunk, muskrat, and lots of prairie dogs. These "dogs" are members of the ground squirrel family, and they were pests in field and garden.

It was not just a matter of an individual hole-in-the-ground home, but they lived in towns of such homes. Around each hole would be a hard-packed mound of earth which served a dual purpose. It kept water from running into their homes, and it served as a porch on which to sit and look around and bark any time there was anyone or anything they didn't like. The prairie dogs also cut the vegetation down for yards around their holes so grass or grain would be mowed over quite an area in a field where they set up their town.

It was not strange that Cousin Charlie feared the Indians had attacked Alden's family, for the alarm had grown with the passing months and no doubt he had heard talk about it. There was real trouble brewing among the Indians. Sitting Bull, Short Bull, and Kicking Bear were some of the leaders, or chiefs, endeavoring to arouse their people against the white people.

Sitting Bull was well known for his oratorical ability, and this talent was being used in an effort to get his people aroused, organized, and prepared to make an attack on the settlers early the next year. But mere rumors were not enough to warrant the government ordering the soldiers into action against the Indians, so they were being watched closely in an effort to find out just what their plans were.

It was against the law for the whites to sell, trade, or give liquor to the Indians, but some unscrupulous men would do it anyway. They traded liquor and guns for the Indian ponies, and thus the red men were enabled to arm themselves with the white man's weapons.

As Alden brought Lydia and Dora from Oelrichs to spend a weekend at home, Dora asked him to take her organ along when he took them back to town, and he agreed to do so. He found someone to help him load it into the wagon, and when they reached Oelrichs, a man who was staying at the Davis hotel helped him unload it and carry it into the house.

> *Not long after this, the girls were awakened one night to find a man was climbing into their bedroom, through a window.*

Not long after this, the girls were awakened one night to find a man was climbing into their bedroom, through a window.

"Get out or I'll shoot!" Dora yelled at him as soon as she realized what had awakened her.

"You haven't got a gun," Lydia informed her aunt—and the intruder as well—so of course Dora's threat did not have its intended effect.

But Dora was more than a match for the man, anyway, fighting him off and sending him on his way with his face badly scratched, even though Lydia had deserted her and crawled under the bed.

At first it was thought that their unwelcome guest might have been one of the soldiers from the ninth cavalry stationed nearby, but later, after Mrs. Davis told them the fellow who had helped unload the organ had left her hotel and the town the next morning after the incident, with his face badly scratched, it was quite evident who had entered their room. Undoubtedly he had seen that the young girl and her aunt were living there alone.

Soldiers were stationed in various places about the Indian reservations because they would be needed in case the Indians caused trouble, and also they were there to prevent trouble if possible.

The Pine Ridge Indian Reservation was not far east from the Pettegrew claim. Included in this reservation was a large part of the River Badlands. The Badlands were so named because the area is made up of steep hills and gullies, ridges and mounds, towers and columns—a strange-looking, misshapen land that is difficult to travel over, and in which there is not much plant life.

Normally one could not see the Badlands from the Pettegrew place, but there were times when a mirage appeared which showed them quite clearly. On a nice clear morning this mirage was often seen, and sometimes they could see the home of the Fisher family who lived four miles away— on the South Dakota/Nebraska state line—in this same way, by mirage.

Alden sometimes made trips to the Black Hills after lumber and Suwano went with him on one of these trips to visit the cousins. It took them two days to travel from their home to where Selby lived north of Hot Springs.

While there Suwano had a good time visiting, playing, and climbing around on the hills with Pearl and Roland. They enjoyed rolling some quite large rocks down the slopes and doing other things in that area so different from the open prairie. On the way back home, they stopped in Hot Springs.

Suwano had some money of her own that she had earned by herding stock for Uncle Charlie along with her own herd during the summer months, so now she went shopping. She bought some material for a dress for herself and another piece of material for her mother. May undoubtedly appreciated the thought behind Suwano's generosity, but she always seemed to think most about the best interests of others, and so it was in this case. She told Suwano that she should have spent all the money on material for her own dress and thus had a better dress for herself.

Suwano's pet rooster was now quite grown up, so Alden decided it was time for him to take a hand in the situation. "I guess I will have to trade Biddy for another rooster," he told her.

"But, Pa," she remonstrated, "Biddy is mine. I don't want you to do that!"

"Well, then," he said, "suppose we go together, you and I, and take Biddy over to the Pickett's. There we can trade him for another rooster, and you can have that one instead."

This idea didn't appeal to her, either, but she began to realize that her father meant this as something he thought must be done. She didn't want to do it, but finally she agreed to it.

"All right, I'll go get Biddy."

They picked out a pretty white rooster from Pickett's flock, and Suwano named him Whitey. Of course, he was not tame like Biddy was, so he didn't really take his place in Suwano's thinking, but she thought him better than no chicken at all.

Then one day he came up missing. She didn't see Whitey with the other chickens, so she began looking for him. She looked all around the farm but could find no trace of him. Finally she thought of looking into an unused well which had been covered over with boards. There she found Whitey and another chicken which had fallen in, and both of them were drowned.

Of course, she was sad about her loss, but she had happy memories of her experience raising Biddy, and she still had Emmy.

Eventually the government secured reliable information about the conspiracy among the Indians. The knowledge that an attack against the whites was planned provided good reason for ordering the military into action. Soldiers were sent to find the Indian leaders and arrest them. This winter of 1890–1891 was another mild winter with little snow or extremely cold weather. It was in December that the soldiers started carrying out this order. One of the Indian leaders was arrested, another one was killed while resisting arrest, and the rest of them escaped into the Badlands with their warriors and their families. The troops were ordered to go after them and bring them out.

At Wounded Knee Creek in the Badlands a captured group of Indians were being searched for weapons when a scuffle occurred between an Indian and a couple of soldiers. This little incident developed into the dreadful and infamous Wounded Knee Massacre, where about 200 Indian warriors and their wives and children were killed and buried there in a trench.

Survivors carried the word to the other Indians and hostilities continued for about a month before it was finally settled. This so-called Messiah War and the Wounded Knee Massacre marked the end of disturbances of any import between the Indians and the whites.

Chapter 12

Lydia's Independence

Selby brought a load of lumber down from the Black Hills to his homestead and began building a house there. Jim also brought a load and helped his father-in-law with the construction. After they had started work on the building, Mr. Evans, the nearest neighbor, came over where they were working.

"Mr. Barnes," he said, "I wouldn't build here if I were you. I have seen water eighteen inches deep over this place where you are building your house."

"That is hard to believe," Selby replied. He took time to look the chosen spot over again more carefully and decided it would be impossible for water to cover it. There was a high bank between it and the nearby creek, so he thought perhaps Mr. Evans just did not want him to build his house so near to the Evan's residence. He dismissed the friendly warning, and went ahead with his work, but he, too, had things to learn about this country.

Early in the spring of 1891 Selby was ready to move his family into the one-room house he had built on the homestead. Here he tells the story of his first attempt to do this:

"We loaded up a wagon with lumber and household goods, and with our stock, we started out. But when we got to the Cheyenne River, we found that it was too high to cross, so we camped there for the night.

"A fellow came riding up to the crossing that evening as we were preparing for the night and introduced himself. His name was Hughes. He, too, decided to wait until morning, so camped there with us.

"The next morning Mr. Hughes was up early, saddled his horse, and rode across the river. He then called to me from the far shore, saying that he thought it was safe to cross, and if I would come over now, he would help us pull the wagon out on the other side, as it was very muddy along the bank there. So, without taking time to finish my breakfast coffee, I went to hitch up my team, and we started across.

"Everything went all right at the start, but before we were fifty feet out in the water my team went out of sight. They came up again, but apparently one horse could not get free from the quicksand. Her hind legs seemed caught in it.

"I saw that her struggles would soon upset the wagon and spill everything into the river if something could not be done quickly, so I called to Hughes for help, then jumped into the water to hold the horse's heads out until he arrived. The struggling horse would raise herself up in front and then throw her weight onto her front feet in an effort to pull her hind legs free. Every time she did this, we both went to the bottom, but after Hughes arrived, we managed to cut this horse free from the wagon. Then she was able to get out of the sand by herself, and floated away down the river.

"With Mr. Hughes help, I got the wagon out of the river onto the bank where we had started from, and then he went on his way, while I set out to find a horse. I was unsuccessful in this, so finally decided to hitch up a two-year-old unbroken colt I had along, and then we went back home."

About a week later Selby tried again, and this time made it through the river and on to their homestead.

Life was often very hard for a pioneer woman of the Dakotas, for most of them were raising large families in small and roughly constructed homes, with few possessions and sometimes without sufficient food and clothing. Many of these women worked out in the fields some of the time, just as May often had done, besides the work in their homes.

May was by now well acquainted with this kind of life. She was always ready and willing at all times to do whatever might be within her power to do for her loved ones and also for others outside the family circle in their times of need. And she continued learning new ways to manage things, coping with new emergencies as they came along, so that her resourcefulness grew with experience through the years.

Although learning much in the school of life, she still felt that an education was of great importance and was most anxious that her children have more opportunities in this field than she had in her early years. In this way, she also wanted them to be prepared for whatever their lot in life might be.

To make the best of things as they were, and to do the best she could, this had become her creed. Often she found there were things that could be done to make things better; yet she also knew it was foolish to waste time and energy fretting about it when things could not be changed or improved. She was not inclined to be worrying or complaining but kept her sense of humor and love of life.

In those earlier times when there were no radios, the womenfolks often sang as they worked about their homes. May enjoyed singing pleasant and cheerful songs about home and country, and also hymns, and the girls took up this good habit from her example as they grew older.

The children all thought their mother did wonderful things, and Ernest said he thought she was the best cook in the country. She was a good cook and made very good bread. Other women often asked for her bread recipe, and no one made better butter than that which she made and sold. The merchants were glad to get her butter, for they knew that it was always good.

When Ernest found out that his uncle, Charlie, had decided to sell the Indian pony, he went at once to his father to ask if they could buy it. Certainly a pony would be an asset for the children in their work herding the cattle, and Suwano was hoping, too, that Alden would agree to buy the pony.

Much to their delight, Alden agreed to make Charlie an offer.

"You can tell him that I will give him a cow and a calf in trade for the pony," he told Ernest, and then added, "or else a cow and five dollars."

Suwano went along with Ernest that evening when he went to see Charlie and tell him about the offer. But Ernest had either misunderstood or became excited at the prospect of having a pony, for he offered Charlie the cow, the calf, *and* the five dollars—all three.

Charlie accepted the offer, and Alden let the deal go through that way, so the children got their pony at last. Later on, their father decided the pony had indeed been worth all that Ernest had offered for it. Her name was Stella.

Horses were a necessity in those days, for the machine age was only in its bud and would not become part of everyday life for years to come. Not only were horses needed for plowing, cultivating, and harvesting, as well as hauling things to and from the markets and railroads, but they were the means of transporting people from place to place by wagon, cart, and carriage. To children the most important use for horses was riding, and in general they were used much like today's individuals use a car, as if it were a necessity to hop into one for transportation even for very short distances.

Ernest and Lydia had learned to ride in Nebraska, and Suwano had some riding experience from going with Ernest on Selim sometimes, but with Stella to ride, it was no longer necessary to utilize the big workhorse for this purpose. Learning to ride was an experience of importance in the lives of most children, something that they looked forward to with pleasant anticipation.

A garden was another necessity, one even more important than transportation. The food supply for the home depended largely upon each family growing as much of it as possible right on the farm. There was often too little money to buy much from the stores.

The Pettegrew family worked on a garden each year. They had an early garden which turned out well if the weather did not get too dry, and in addition they had a larger area where corn, potatoes, and sometimes other crops were planted.

This larger garden was on a five-acre plot north of the house which Alden plowed and prepared for planting. Then it was up to May and the children to do most of the planting and hoeing. There was always the threat that a hailstorm might destroy all their hard work, but when the gardens turned out well, it made their efforts all seem worthwhile, through good years and bad years.

The potato bug was still around as it had been when Melissa May and her little brother Robert had worked in the garden helping their grandfather pick them off the potato vines. But now it was Mary and Lou who carried on this task. They helped their father gather the bugs by knocking them off the vines into cans, and after the bugs were gathered, Alden would see to it that they were destroyed.

This was tedious work, and the hot sun helped to make the task more disagreeable, but the bugs would eat the vines up if they were not destroyed. There were no sprays to use on them, but a poisonous substance called Paris Green could be bought and put out which would kill these beetles. However, when people could not afford to buy this poison, they still had to gather the bugs and burn them.

A small garden put in near a well or creek could be watered, but the little creek on the claim went dry in summer. Some folks who lived along Horsehead Creek irrigated and had fine gardens most every year.

Alden had some sugar beets in the larger garden that year, and later on Suwano had the task of feeding them to a cow they were fattening for beef. She fed some of them to her Emmy too.

With Selby's children in the community, there were more school-age children, so a spring term was held with Lucinda Pettegrew as teacher. One day the children heard horses, and, looking out the schoolroom window, saw a white horse running straight toward the school as if it were going to come right in through the window. Behind it came Charlie Pettegrew on a bay horse.

The horses went around and around the schoolhouse, as Charlie attempted to head the white one toward home. Finally they left, with Nellie, the white horse, headed toward Alden's place and Charlie following after on the other one.

When they reached the long house, they began going around and around it just as they had the schoolhouse. Charlie called to Mary, who was inside the house with Lou, and tried to persuade her to come out and help him head the horse off, but Mary was afraid that the white horse would run over her, so she would not go out to help her uncle.

After a while, Nellie started off toward home, and the game was over.

The school in Oelrichs was a two-room school, Dora teaching one room and a man teaching the other one. John Critie McKee and Dora Pettegrew soon became good friends, and then began keeping company. After school closed for the summer vacation they were married.

Soon afterward Dora came out with her husband so he could meet those of her family whom he had not already met.

"Where are Lou and Mary?" Dora asked.

"Oh, they're out playing somewhere," May answered.

"I'll go hunt them up then, for I want Critie to see them too."

She found them where they had wandered, wearing their little chambray sunbonnets for protection from the sun, as it was a hot summer day.

One day the children heard horses, and, looking out the schoolroom window, saw a white horse running straight toward the school as if it were going to come right in through the window.

May made these sunbonnets for the girls, and sometimes she made them from tea straw. The children went barefoot most of the summer, and seldom had opportunity to go anywhere outside the immediate neighborhood. As long as they stayed around home, in the yard, on paths, or in the road, they did not have to worry about stepping on cactus or being bothered much by snakes.

May not only made all the girls' clothing, but she made shirts and overcoats for Alden and Ernest as well. She knitted mittens and scarves, made the curtains, rugs, and such things for her home and had begun doing sewing for others outside the home again, as she had before in Nebraska.

Instead of coming home to stay after the close of school in Oelrichs, Lydia stayed there and began working out.

She was only thirteen, but she thought of herself as a young lady now, not a child anymore, and to her younger sisters at home she seemed like a grown-up lady too.

May's eldest daughter had a ready smile and a quick temper. She was interested in religious things because of May's careful teaching, but she loved a good time most of all—to have fun, laugh, be happy, and dance. Her intention was to have both religion and a good time.

She worked first at Hunt's rooming house where she did housework such as washing dishes and helping take care of rooms. Mr. and Mrs. Hunt took a drive out from town one Sunday and brought Lydia home for a short visit with her family, and her cousin Roland went in to visit her quite often at the rooming house.

Later in the summer Lydia went to work for Mrs. Davis at the hotel. Along the way, between the family homes and the town, Roland had tacked up advertisements of a patent medicine he was selling. A fellow who stayed at the hotel had noticed them and liked to tease Lydia about it. He told her that he saw an advertisement on the side of the Oelrichs bridge about Doctor Barnes' remedy, with headquarters in the Davis kitchen.

Crops turned out very well this year, and that helped renew the settler's confidence in the country. Those who had been able to stick it out through the Indian trouble and the drought had learned much more about what might be expected, and what crops were likely to do best on the high plains. They had learned something about the weather, the soil, the hazards, and the risks involved in living there.

Grain did not do as well there as it had on the homestead in Nebraska, but the area seemed more suited as grazing land for cattle. Some who had stayed on were able to buy up land from those who left and thus start building a ranch large enough to support cattle.

Alden farmed about forty-five acres of his land; most of the rest of it was used for pasture. Selby, too, tried farming, but he found that he could do better as a carpenter and doing general blacksmith work.

Suwano liked it when she could take her herd of cattle along Horsehead Creek near Selby's homestead because then she was able to spend some of the time playing with Pearl while the cattle grazed. After the herd law was revoked, however, it was no longer necessary to herd the cattle. Then people had to fence their crops to protect them, for cattle and horses were turned loose on the range and left to wander freely wherever they wished.

In the late afternoon or early evening each day the cows had to be found and brought in for milking if they were not already at home. Suwano usually rode the pony, Stella, to round up the cows, but girls did not ride astride horses then as they do now.

She went after the cows one evening with only a strap around Stella's body to hang onto, instead of a saddle. She didn't know it, but she was riding for a fall.

As they went by the Pickett place, where weeds had grown tall since the family had moved away, Jack suddenly appeared, coming through the weeds to the road. This startled the pony, so she jumped forward, and Suwano fell off. She was slightly stunned at first, so lay there a short while. Thinking that Stella had probably run off and maybe gone back home, she imagined that the folks would come running to see if she was hurt.

But she soon felt all right, looked around, and found that she was lying right behind the pony, which was just standing there. Stella had her head turned and was looking at Suwano, as if wondering what she would do next, and waiting to see if she would get up. So, get up she did, and back on the pony, and off they went to get the cows, just as if nothing had happened.

Stella was an ideal pony for children to ride. She was always careful, and tried not to lose her riders, but if she did, she would stand and wait for them to get back on.

It was August and time to go plumming. May knew the plums would be ripe in the slate hills at the edge of Plains Valley, and she wanted to get some of them. Fruit was scarce and they would be a welcome addition to their food supply. Hattie and her family were now living on the Pickett place, so Alden agreed to take May, his sister, and some of the children on a plumming excursion. The plums were more than thirty miles away, so it was to be a camping trip, with Suwano along to take care of the two babies while their mothers picked plums. Baby Carrie was almost a year old now, and Hattie's baby, also named Carrie, was somewhat younger. They called her Little Carrie.

"Bring me the largest plum you find, will you, George?" were the last words they heard as they started out. It was Ernest who made this request, and George did not forget.

As they neared home on the return trip, George jumped out of the wagon and ran ahead, getting to the house before the others did. Ernest saw him coming.

"Did you bring that plum for me?" he asked.

His cousin took a big plum out of his mouth before answering.

"Yep, I sure did," he answered finally, holding out the plum. "Here it is."

"Well, what did you have it in your mouth for?" Ernest stood looking at it.

"So I wouldn't lose it," George replied.

Ernest took the plum, washed it carefully, and then ate it. After all, they didn't get much fresh fruit, so he thought it shouldn't be wasted.

May made preserves and jelly from the plums they brought home and also dried some of them.

The so-called Gay Nineties were not very gay for some who lived on the prairie of western South Dakota. There was no merry whirl or mad rush of church, school, club, and business activities, yet life was not always as drab and dull as one might think.

There were events of a social nature and some which combined business with pleasure. Young folks in the community found opportunity to meet with their friends and acquaintances by attending Sunday school and any other community gatherings held in the little log schoolhouse. The regular Sunday school was directed by Mr. Brook, a farmer/preacher/teacher member of the community who adhered to the Christian Church faith, generally called Campbellite.

Perhaps some youths picked up a little religion by attending such meetings, even though they may not have had much of any religious training at home. Others were more serious and sincere, but not all of them had been brought up as May's children were with a sound fundamental faith in the Holy Scriptures.

She always believed what the Bible had to say, regardless of what men might add to it, subtract from it, or interpret it to mean. Her faith was not based upon the established interpretation of any organized church body: not on Sunday school attendance or membership in a church. But her reverence for the Bible as the Word of God seemed to be the basis of her faith, and she based the home training of her children upon what she knew of the Bible, often telling Bible stories to the children when they were small.

Mr. Brook was the leader of most all local religious activities, but he was inclined to ridicule all religious beliefs a great deal, except, of course, his own.

Alden and May did not attend Sunday school, but they allowed the older children to go. Ernest, Lydia, and Suwano attended quite regularly and took Mary along with them a few times. Previously, while living in Plains Valley, the Pettegrews had become acquainted with the Methodist circuit-riding minister of the area whose name was Tuttie. He went to the little valley as often as he could and preached on Sunday in May's living room where as many as were interested would gather to hear him.

Mr. Tuttie lived in Oelrichs and was pastor of the Methodist church there. Occasionally he drove out to the little log schoolhouse to hold a meeting at three o'clock Sunday afternoon.

As her young folks left the house on their way to attend one of these Sunday afternoon meetings, May told Suwano to invite the Reverend home to spend the night with them. Suwano did as her mother instructed, and Mr. Tuttie brought her home in his cart.

That evening Mr. Brook was going to preach, so Alden and May decided to go and take Mr. Tuttie along with them to hear Mr. Brook.

When he saw the Methodist minister there, Mr. Brook decided to speak on the subject of baptism. He talked and talked about this and read where Paul speaks of being "buried with him by baptism," in Romans 6:4.

After they got home from the meeting, Mr. Tuttie sat by the table thinking over what had been said.

"Well, if it would say 'buried with Him *in* baptism,' I would be an immersionist," he said.

Suwano had recently memorized the Bible verse which does say just that, so she got out her Bible and looked up the text. Then she handed it to her mother, who in turn gave it to Mr. Tuttie to read. The text was Colossians 2:12, and he read it.

"Hmmm—it does say 'in,' doesn't it?" was his only comment.

But sometime later, after Mr. Tuttie had left Oelrichs and was somewhere in the Black Hills, they heard that he had changed his religious connections and had become a member of the Baptist church.

During the preaching service which followed Mr. Brook's Sunday school, he was the speaker, and he would have his son George act as a deacon for it. George passed out the communion dressed in his cowboy outfit with spurs on his boots and a six-shooter in his holster. This seemed entirely out of place in a church service, since he could easily have taken them off before serving without any danger of needing them before the close of the services!

Lou taught the local school again as she had in the spring, and Mary began attending for the first time. She got very tired from sitting still so long and decided to stand up in her seat for a while, but soon learned she could not get any such special favors from her aunt. Louise Mathwig and Mary were about the same age and soon became good friends at school.

Lydia had returned home after nearly a year in Oelrichs so she could attend the home school that fall. She was fun-loving and liked to have company. Most every Sunday afternoon she had young folks coming to her home for a good time together. Sometimes they played games in the yard.

Roland and Pearl were usually there on these occasions, and often the young folks of the Brook family came, too—Ellen, Nellie, and Talitha and their brothers George and Charlie. For one of the games they liked to play a ball was used, and they dug a hole in the ground for a goal. Then they chose sides, and each player got a stick. One side would try to get the ball into the hole, while the other side would try to keep it out. The younger children liked to be included in this game too.

Lydia was rather small and wanted to stay that way, so Ernest thought it was fun to tease her about it by telling her that she would become a big lummox like Ma! He did not realize how uncomplimentary this was for his mother but was only intent on disturbing Lydia with his remark.

Chapter 13

Another Milestone

Sometimes when Father Pettegrew was away from home overnight, May would send one of the girls to stay with their grandmother so she would not have to be alone at night. Suwano had often been the one to go, but she thought it was awfully lonesome there with just the two of them alone, and she hardly knew what to do. It was very different than at home where there were always children about to play with. She would sit beside the straw stack, on the sunny side, to play alone sometimes, and her only playmate there was the dog.

Mary, too, had stayed with her grandmother overnight sometimes, but Lou had never yet had this privilege, and somehow it seemed to her that it would be a special treat or an adventure to be allowed to go. She wanted very much to stay with her grandmother sometime like the others had.

The day finally came when she was given permission to go, and Suwano took her there on the pony when she went to get the cows in the evening, leaving her there to stay overnight.

Everything went fine until Grandmother had to go out to the cave to get milk and butter, leaving Lou all alone. This was just too much for her. When Grandmother returned, she found Lou sitting by the stove with her sunbonnet on, crying. She was ready to return home.

Then Mother Pettegrew told her little granddaughter that she was glad to have her come to stay but not if she was going to cry about it. That just would not do at all. After supper was over, Lou enjoyed listening to her grandmother's stories of when she was a little girl, and tried to forget how homesick she was, but in the morning she was up bright and early and soon ready and waiting to go home.

The girls all enjoyed the stories their grandmother told during the evenings when they stayed with her, one by one. These were stories about her own life when she was a child. Her home had been in Cincinnati, Ohio, during her earliest years.

She told of a flood which occurred during that time, in which many people were drowned, and they could see horses and other animals and all kinds of household things floating by on the river. A cradle was seen floating along, and fearing that there might be a baby in it, some men took a boat and went out to get it. Sure enough, there was a little girl in the cradle, not harmed in the least, so they took her ashore. Her parents were never found, so it was thought that the rest of the family had been drowned.

Then there was the cholera plague. The people who lived next door to her family had a little girl just about her age with whom she played a lot, and they had many good times together. One day they played until quite late in the evening. The next morning her parents told her that her little playmate was dead. She had died in the night from cholera.

> *Grandfather was thus taken away one time, and Grandmother said that she never expected to see him again.*

A minister left Cincinnati on horseback during this time to hold some meetings elsewhere, and the next day a man set out after him to tell him that his family had all died from cholera. When the messenger reached the place where the minister was to hold meetings, he found that the minister was dead also. So many died in so short a time that it was hard to find men to dig graves in which to bury them, and they had to be buried without any services.

Grandmother had a brother in Cincinnati who was operating a store in partnership with another man. One evening the other fellow went home early and then later her brother thought of something he wanted to see his partner about, so he stopped by his house on the way home. The man was dying of cholera. This experience frightened her brother, and they all feared the plague, but none of the family got it.

Many years later, during the Civil War, after Grandmother had a family of her own, they were living near the border between the North and South where there was much trouble. Sometimes when the Northern troops were near, they would take anyone they thought sympathized with the South and shoot them. Then when the Southern troops were there, they would do the same thing to anyone they thought sympathized with the North.

Grandfather was thus taken away one time, and Grandmother said that she never expected to see him again. The leader of the group of soldiers who took him away made him get up behind him on his horse, and off they went. Grandfather fully expected to be shot, but as they went along, he happened to think of giving the Mason sign, and this troop leader was a Mason, so he told Grandfather to get down and go back home.

These were some of the stories which Mother Pettegrew told May's girls.

Alden made many trips to the timber for wood, of course, and May decided to go with him on one of these trips, so she left the girls at Selby's while she was away. Roland came over to stay with Ernest at home.

During her absence a big wind came up. It blew the stovepipe down from Selby's house, and a blacksmith bellows was blown up onto the roof. The windstorm frightened the younger children, and they began to cry, fearing that the house was going to be blown down.

But as soon as the wind died down, they forgot their fears and had a good time playing together.

The Christmas of 1892 was also a memorable day for May's children. The family gathering was held at Selby's home where a big dinner was served, and they had a Christmas tree with gifts. Selby played the part of Santa in passing out the packages. Dora and her husband were there, and Selby felt badly about it when he found that there was no gift under the tree for them. Afterward he got something for them and gave it to them later when they again visited his family.

This winter there was more snow than there had been the two previous years. Mary and Lou were always glad when it snowed and the wind piled it up in big drifts, for then they could slide down the drifts. One would have the scoop shovel and the other a big discarded dishpan, and what fun they had sliding on the snow!

It was difficult to haul water from the well when there was a lot of snow on the ground, so May often filled the wash boiler and large kettles with snow and melted it on the stove to get water for washing.

The snow piled up high on the door to the cave, so it had to be dug away before they could get potatoes and other vegetables which were stored there for winter use.

If anything went wrong at night among the cattle, Jack would come to the house and bark to wake someone up. As soon as anyone got up to find out what was wrong, Jack would go toward the barn. If they did not come right out, he would go back to the house and repeat his act.

He did this during one very cold night when no one wanted to go out. Perhaps they reasoned that it likely was not anything serious. Anyway, Alden and Ernest both disregarded the alarm and Jack did not get anyone to answer. It was not such a stormy night, but whatever their reasons for not heeding the dog's call, it was not a false alarm. In the morning, they found that a yearling had become caught in the door and was frozen to death. Jack had done all he could to save her life.

Early in 1892, nearly a year after he moved down from the Black Hills to his homestead, Selby came to realize the sincerity of Mr. Evans' friendly warning about high water on the flat where he had chosen to build his home.

A late snow, nearly a foot deep, was followed by a thaw which melted the snow in ten or twelve hours. Selby was not at home when the flash flood reached the flat. He was on the other side of Horsehead Creek and could not get across it because of the high water.

His family had to wade out of their home and get onto higher ground but could not take much with them.

"The only way I could get even with Evans for having told me that he had seen eighteen inches of water over that area was to tell him that I had seen it four feet deep right in my house," Selby was later to remark.

A hen with baby chicks had been taken inside the house in a tub, and they were thus quite safe during the brief flood because they floated around on the water until it receded much like the ark did in the days of Noah. But a rooster did not fare so well. He chose a haystack as his refuge, and the haystack was swept away by the waters. He was last seen, atop the stack, crowing lustily as it floated away down the stream.

Selby had two yoke of oxen, and soon after the flood waters passed on downstream, he used them to move his house onto higher ground. He also moved houses for other people with the oxen.

Seasonal rains usually filled many low places with water for a short period of time. One such area was a quite large flat piece of ground which was surrounded by higher land, so that when it was filled with water it resembled a lake, and that was what folks called it—the lake. Water remained in it longer than it did in other places.

The lake was not far from May's house. In the spring when water was in it, mosquitoes became a real nuisance. The horses would go running through the water in an effort to get rid of the pests, splashing it over themselves. Then Alden would build a smudge in the barnyard so when the horses came there, they learned to stand near the smoke, and that would drive the mosquitoes away from them.

This time when the lake was drying up and the water getting stale, it seemed as if it produced toads. Small toads appeared everywhere. They were in the yards, and on the roads, and constantly under foot. It seemed one could hardly take a step anywhere outside without the risk of stepping on a little toad. The wagon wheels would smash them, and May had quite a time trying to keep them out of the cave where she kept her milk and butter.

Suwano and Mary enjoyed pretending the toads were cattle, and they staged roundups with them, building pens to keep them in. But, of course, they could not make them stay inside the pens for very long.

When the water was all gone and the weather became warmer, those toads all seemed to disappear suddenly. No one knew what became of them.

Since coming to South Dakota, their herd of milk cows had increased considerably. Most of the cream May would make into butter to sell, so they would not have much of that for their own use, but there was skim milk and buttermilk, too, and she made cottage cheese for their own use too. Then she began making brick cheese. Thinking it would be a good idea to make it in large enough amounts so they could sell it, too, she went to work to make what she would need for this project.

Some improvements had been made by the settlers, and more were in process of being made. Selby built a sod room and joined it onto his one-room frame house, and this addition was used for a bedroom. Alden bought a house from a family who had moved away, planning to move it onto his claim soon. Near where their new house would be situated, he built a small sod house to be used for a milk house.

In this, May built a long table over which she placed a mosquito netting covered frame, and under this frame, on the table, the pans of milk were set so the cream would rise to the top. Then she would skim it off and put it into the churn.

Churning the cream until the butter came—or separated itself from the liquid—became a task for the younger children which they soon began to dislike very much. They would get so very tired of the monotonous task and wish for it to be finished quickly so they could do something more active.

In making what she needed for her cheese-making project, May used her supply of ingenuity. She was good at making, fixing, and doing many things and so also was her brother Selby.

It was Selby who made the tank, or vat, for her. This was like a big tank but built especially to fill the requirements of cheese making. It sloped along the bottom, and he installed a faucet at the lower end.

May strained the milk into this vat, and let it set awhile to thicken. She added rennet and coloring, stirred it in well, and as the milk thickened and separated, she drained off all the whey she could get out through the faucet at the end of the vat. When there was no more liquid in the mass in the vat, she would divide it into separate amounts, each to become a five-pound cheese after pressing.

The barrel-like part of her cheese press was the right size to hold three of these cheeses at one time. Each one was wrapped in cheesecloth, put into the press with a board fitted on top, and then the top of the press was tightened so the moisture would all get pressed out and each cheese would be held firmly in shape until they became hardened and dry enough to take out.

Next she would sew each cheesecloth tightly around the cheese, paint them with wax, and place them up on a shelf in the milk house to cure. In a few weeks they would be ready to eat.

In the early spring when the cows had plenty of new grass to feed on, May would have to skim more cream off the milk before trying to make cheese. If she did not, it would be too rich, and the cheese would crumble.

A sad accident took place over at the Evans home that summer. Selby's younger children were there playing with the Evans children, when Mrs. Evans suddenly realized that her baby, Willie, who was about two years old, was not anywhere in sight. She asked the children if they knew where the baby was, but they told her they had not seen him, so she started to look around for him.

After having looked most everywhere else she could think of, she went to the well, and looking down, saw his feet sticking up out of the water.

While Charlie Barnes went to call Mr. Evans from the field where he was working, the mother got a long two-by-four, thinking she might be able to slide down it into the well to get the baby, but she gave up the idea. If she had tried, she, too, might have been drowned as the baby already was.

Pearl came to tell the Pettegrews about what had happened, and May was called on to "lay the body out" as they called it—to make the burial gown and dress the body for burial. This was just another of the many services she performed for others in their time of need.

Dora's first child, Mary, was born that summer, and Lydia went to work for her aunt awhile, doing housework and helping care for the baby.

Selby helped Alden in moving the Neff house to its new location. The whole building was too large for the wagons, so they took one section, which had been added as a lean-to room, away from the main building and moved it first. The other section was brought over afterward and put into place where it was to remain, then the lean-to section was pulled up to be joined back onto it.

The children were much interested in this moving process. Suwano went inside and watched from an upstairs window as the lean-to was pulled into place in the late afternoon.

As time permitted, the work was continued. The house had to be leveled, and the extra room joined back onto it, before the cleaning could be done on the inside. This was not a large house, for there were only three rooms, two downstairs and one upstairs, but it was much more like a real house than the long one in which they had been living since they came to South Dakota.

To May, getting and moving into this house seemed like another milestone in their second pioneering period. The progress of this "beginning all over again" had been delayed by the months spent in Plains Valley, but now things were beginning to improve.

It would be some time before they could get the inside of their "new" house finished, but they moved in, leaving the lathing and plastering to be done later, and the long house was torn down. The lumber from it was used in the construction of other buildings or adding to those already built.

Emmy, the calf which Suwano had bought from her father for fifty cents, was now about two years old and quite grown up. While the cattle were being watered at the well one day, Emmy got crowded up against the fence, and some of the other cows hooked her with their horns. She was badly injured, and died from the wounds, so that was the end of Suwano's first venture into the cattle business.

Sometimes when Alden and May had to be away overnight, Charlie would come to stay with the children and help Ernest with the milking. At sixteen, Ernest thought himself almost a man, and he liked to pit his strength against Charlie's by "rassling" with him. This occasionally became quite rough, and whenever they indulged in this sport in the corral, Renie, a cow which had become quite attached to Ernest, would come to his aid.

Renie acted as if she feared that Ernest would get hurt, so she would take after Charlie and break up the fight.

The children were all out at the corral one evening and Cousin Pearl was there with them. Ernest started walking about inside the corral, and Renie began to follow him, so Pearl picked up baby Carrie and put her on Renie's back so she could have a ride. Pearl walked along beside the cow, holding Carrie there while the cow followed Ernest around and around inside the corral, and Carrie thought she had a fine ride.

Most of the cows had horns, but Renie didn't have any. Some cows were real bossy, and one cow named Cherry often stood in the entrance to the cowshed, refusing to let certain others go in at all. Then Renie would have to stay outside. However, if she could run or sneak in past Cherry, and get beside a cow whose name was Pied, who also had long horns, but was not mean, then Renie would be safe. Pied would not let the others be mean to Renie when she was near.

But after a while Pied was injured by a mule kicking her, and she stayed out on a hillside alone, because she was too badly hurt to come home. While she was there, Renie didn't pay any attention to Ernest; her concern was all for Pied. She would go over in the direction of Pied and bawl to her as if sympathizing with her, and after Pied's death, mourned her loss in the same way for a while.

Then her attention returned to Ernest, and her liking for him increased. She would sometimes go bawling and looking for him! If Ernest had the dog with him when he drove the cows out in the morning, Renie came running back to chase Jack away from Ernest, as if she was either jealous of Jack or thought that Ernest needed to be protected from him.

When Ernest rode after the cows, to bring them in for the evening milking, he often took Mary with him, having her ride behind him on Stella. She enjoyed this favor from her big brother, and the experience helped her in learning to ride by herself later on.

> *Lydia and Suwano worked in this little store some of the time, waiting on customers and keeping things in order.*

The lean-to section of the new home was the kitchen, and one end of it was reserved for a little country store where they sold the butter and cheese May made as well as other staple groceries.

Lydia and Suwano worked in this little store some of the time, waiting on customers and keeping things in order. It seemed to be a good arrangement and they were doing well with it until Alden began taking hay in payment for groceries.

He was raising some black poll steers, and had bought more, enough to make up a carload, so planned to fatten them and ship them to Omaha later. He needed more hay as feed for them, but some of the hay traded to him had too much old dead grass in it, full of alkali, and fifteen head of his cattle died from eating it. That was such a big loss that they had to quit the store.

Chapter 14

A Fight

Jack had learned to shake hands with people, but he was never a very friendly dog. He would not allow anyone on the place who carried a cattle whip. The place and the people living on it were under his protective care, so he would not take any chances and was always on guard.

Although he was very loyal to his family, there was one time when Lydia did not count upon this loyalty—not very much, anyway. She had decided to have some fun by scaring Ernest while he was working in the barn one evening. It was dark, so she got one of her mother's sheets and wrapped it around herself to look like a ghost and then started toward the barn, slipping along stealthily toward where Ernest was at work.

But Jack spotted this "ghost" first, and he did not propose to have anything like that around the place, so he started after her. Lydia heard him coming, and now she was the frightened one. She threw off her disguise as quickly as she could, because she knew from having seen him in action that he would take her down savagely if he got to her before he saw who it really was.

If Jack was near when any of the herd began a fight, he would watch until he saw the larger one getting the best of the smaller, then he would take the part of the smaller animal against the other one. It was the same when the children got in any little fights between themselves. Then Jack would take the part of the smaller one or take the part of the girls against Ernest or any other boy. Of course, there was little chance of anyone winning against him, for he was a savage fighter.

One time he got into a fight with another dog larger than himself over a bone and would have badly injured or perhaps killed the other dog had they not been separated.

Selby was quite a storyteller, and he liked most of all to tell ghost stories. As children gather in front of the TV to watch cartoons, westerns, and even horror shows today, then they entertained themselves by reading and telling stories occasionally, and perhaps most of what they had along this line was much better than the usual children's comics of today.

The ghost stories her uncle told, however, and the Indian stories told by some others, were equally frightening to little Lou, although the other children seemed to enjoy listening to them without much fear. When Lou's big blue eyes widened with fright, the others were amused. They told her that her eyes were as big as saucers, and the storytellers enjoyed their storytelling all the more because of this.

A new chicken house was built, a small one which seemed more like a playhouse in size, and this reminded Lydia and Suwano of the fun they had playing in such a small-sized chicken house in Nebraska. They told Mary and Lou about it, so then, of course, the two younger girls wanted to use this new building for a playhouse too. They had a good time playing in it until May found out what they were doing.

The girls were playing inside the house in the daytime, and it was after the hens had been moved into it, so they stayed there at night, but were turned out in the daytime. The girls playing inside prevented the hens from coming in to lay their eggs. Feeling that the girls were old enough to know better than to do this, May gave them each a switching for it.

Jim and Coral Smith stayed on in the Black Hills after Selby moved onto his homestead. There they lost their little daughter Della to scarlet fever, and they also lost a baby son. Now they came down from the hills and moved into a sod house that was standing empty on the Neff place from which Alden had moved the frame house for his own use.

Jim and Coral liked to go to dances and other social affairs frequently, especially dances which were quite often held in the homes. Poole's had another dance, and May had allowed Lydia and Suwano to watch the dancing there, and then Alden and May had held a dance in the long house once.

LaDeau's, who lived about a mile and a half southwest of the Pettegrew's place, had dances in their home a number of times. Jim and Coral attended, sometimes taking Ernest, Lydia, and Suwano with them.

Programs were put on in the schoolhouse occasionally by some enterprising group. These were called Exhibitions. Jim Smith was the leader in getting up one such program in the early fall of 1892. The schoolhouse was considered much too small for this one, so a stage was set on the porch of Alden's new house, and seats were arranged in the yard in front of this stage for the audience.

As it was still summery weather, such an outdoor gathering could be held in the evening quite easily, and a large number of people could attend.

Besides being the principal instigator of the Exhibition, Jim was also one of the leading actors. Charlie was in it, too, but Jim was colored up, blackened to play the part of a Negro. They had a play, recitations and readings were given, songs were included, and there were jokes. Also someone danced a jig.

Mary and Lou were allowed to stay up for a while, so they could watch the early part of the program. They sat in the crowd until May decided it was time for them to go to bed, then they had to leave.

Of course, they did not want to go to bed—and after they were upstairs, they climbed out the window of their room onto the roof of the lean-to kitchen. From there they crawled over onto the roof of the porch which was being used as a stage. They couldn't see the performance from there, of course, but they could watch the group out in front who were watching it, and they enjoyed that anyway.

One pleasant Sunday afternoon Alden and May took Carrie with them and went to visit at Selby's home. Roland came riding up on his white pony, Tressie, to see Ernest.

"Let's go for a ride," he suggested to his cousin. "Go get your pony saddled, and come on."

"All right, I will," Ernest answered, and headed for the corral. Soon they were on their way across the prairie for an enjoyable horseback ride together.

The girls watched them go, and then started thinking of what they might do to make the afternoon more interesting for themselves.

"Let's hitch up old Charlie to the buggy and take a ride," Lydia said brightly. "We might as well get out too."

This they did, and soon they, too, were on their way across the prairie for a ride, Suwano and Lydia in the seat, with Mary and Lou sitting behind the seat in the little box-like section there, facing backward.

The boys returned first, before the girls got back, and since it was early evening by then, they were hungry and thought about supper.

"Couldn't we start getting supper ready and surprise the girls with it all done when they come?" Roland suggested.

"Sure," Ernest responded readily. "You can fry the potatoes, and I'll get the table set." So they went to work but kept an eye out for the girls' return.

The buggy came in sight before the boys had supper all ready, so they locked the doors of the kitchen, both the one leading outside and the one to the living room, to keep the girls out until they were ready to let them in to eat the surprise supper.

Lydia stopped the buggy by the house and got out, along with the little girls, to go in the house, leaving Suwano to unhitch the horse and put it in the stable.

Finding the kitchen doors locked was a challenge to Lydia. She didn't know what the boys were up to, but she intended to find out and to get inside just because she was locked out. She went into the living room and got a button hook from a shelf. Lydia would have made a good burglar; she was good at such things as opening locked doors with a button hook.

She got the door unlocked with the little girls standing there watching her do it, and by the time Suwano returned from the barn, the others were going in.

Mary and Lou walked right in, and the boys didn't say anything to them, but Lydia was following, and Suwano, who knew nothing about what was going on nor that the doors had been locked, began to walk right in, too.

Roland grabbed Lydia, intending to put her back out, and Ernest said to Suwano, "You are not coming in here!"

"Well, I'm not going out," Suwano countered. Lydia felt the same way, so the fight was on.

Mary and Lou had thought it was fine that supper was almost ready. The table was all set, and the potatoes frying in a big skillet on the stove gave off an appetizing odor. Lou, always interested in food, was thinking of how good things were going to taste after their ride in the fresh air.

To keep from being put out, Suwano grabbed up some knives and forks from the table with which to defend herself. But Ernest seemed to think that she intended to use them on him, so he knocked them out of her hand, and slapped her on the side of the head. Then she grabbed a saw that was hanging on the wall beside her, and Ernest tried to get it away from her. In the scuffle the saw nicked his ear a bit, so he struck out at her again.

Words were flying, too. Lydia gave Roland a verbal going over, and Suwano ended up by calling her brother a fool.

The little girls watched the fight and were scared that someone was going to get hurt. But Suwano got away from Ernest and ran upstairs, and Lydia got in the last words by telling Roland to go home and never come back again, so it was over.

Suwano did not have Lou's appetite for food and missing a meal did not disturb her very much. Upstairs, she threw herself down on the bed and began to cry. She was quick to realize what she had done—after it was all over. She remembered that in the Bible it says anyone who calls his brother a fool is in danger of hellfire. The family believed that the wicked would burn forever and ever, but this belief was not what bothered Suwano the most. It was the realization that she had done something so very wrong, something which the Bible specifically said not to do, this was what hurt her the most. She felt hurt, frustrated, and sorry about what she had done, because she knew it was wrong.

Roland left, and things calmed down. Lou ate and enjoyed her supper, but perhaps she was the only one who did. The meal was spoiled for most of them and all four who engaged in the incident were much ashamed of themselves after it was all over.

When Alden and May returned, they soon found out about the whole thing from Mary and Lou who could not keep a secret. May gave Ernest a scolding for his part in the affair, and then she scolded Suwano. She was rather disappointed in them for having a fight like that, for she thought that they knew better than to do such a thing.

Roland didn't mention the affair at home, and he came back again soon, just as if nothing had happened like being told "don't ever come back again."

The Methodist minister stationed at Oelrichs since Tuttie left was a Mr. Skaggs, and he came out to the community occasionally as did his predecessor. On one of his trips, he visited in the homes of those who were Methodists, coming last to the Pettegrew home after visiting the others, probably to spend the night there. In the evening, he went out to talk with Alden while he was at work doing the evening chores.

"Mr. Pettegrew," he said, "I am surprised at you for not speaking up in defense of our faith."

"How is that?" Alden asked in surprise.

"Well, one of our sisters," and he gave the name of the lady to whom he referred, "was telling me of Mr. Brook ridiculing the Methodists during a meeting in the schoolhouse, and she said that you just sat there without saying one word."

Alden had nothing at all to say in answer to this accusation.

"Haven't you anything to say for yourself?" the minister asked.

"No."

And as far as Alden was concerned, that was that. The preacher couldn't get him to discuss the matter further, so they went on talking about other things.

May was curious about what had been discussed by the two men that evening, so after Mr. Skaggs had returned to Oelrichs, she sought her first chance to ask Alden about it.

"What was it that Mr. Skaggs had to discuss with you last night?"

"He told me that I should have spoken up in defense of my faith at the meeting when Mr. Brooks was denouncing our church," was the reply. "Someone told him that I just sat there and never said a word."

"Well!" May exclaimed in exasperation, "didn't you tell him that you were not at that meeting at all?"

"No, I did not."

"Why didn't you? I certainly would have."

"I just did not think that would be right," was his reply. "I couldn't have told him that without showing that someone was a liar. I just said nothing so there would not be any trouble."

That was Alden's way—to avoid trouble if he saw it coming and could avoid it as easily as in this instance just by keeping his mouth shut.

Another family went with them when they went plumming this fall. They had been told about the plums and so wanted to go along, and May sent them word when they would be going. There were lots of plums this time, but it rained while they were camped out there, so it wasn't an altogether pleasant excursion. The other family went back afterwards to get more of the plums, and they sold them to other people.

Some kinds of wild fruits could be found in certain places. Both black and yellow wild currants were found along Horsehead Creek, and these were used fresh, in sauce, and in pies. Chokecherry trees grew along the Horsehead, too, and these cherries were eaten raw and made into jelly.

Fruit trees put out by the settlers did not turn out at all well. The Mathwig family had put out quite an orchard of apples, but every year the wind blew the apples off before they ripened. Some fruit was grown in the Black Hills then, but it was not nearly as large or as good as the fruit which they had in Nebraska.

May's older children continued to talk things over with her, for the counsel and suggestions she had to give them was valued in most instances and heeded. However, Lydia was becoming more interested in working away from home where she could get something more for the work she did. To her it seemed that everyone at home benefited from the work she did, but rewards from her work away from home were hers alone. Also she enjoyed being with other people and in other places.

Suwano was more serious and somewhat less fun-loving than Lydia. She was not anxious to become a young lady and go places and do things away from home but was more interested in things on the farm. She had been consistent in her care for her chicken and her calf and proud of the results, even though disappointed with the eventual outcome.

Ernest, Lydia, Suwano, and Mary all attended school that fall. A young woman, Della Borst, was the teacher. Miss Borst was inexperienced and often homesick, but the children all seemed to like her. She taught them some new and different kinds of songs. Lydia invited the teacher to come home with her for dinner one time, for they knew she did not have a very good place to board.

A book agent came by and stopped at the school to give his sales talk to the teacher as he went through the community trying to sell a book entitled *Bible Readings for the Home Circle*.

He didn't make a sale at the school, but when he came to the Pettegrew home, he found an interested listener as he went through his sales talk, for May still wanted to learn more about the Bible.

Although doing her best to live as she believed was right according to what she knew of the Bible and its instructions, and bringing up her children to have the same respect for the Scriptures, there were still a great many things in the Bible that she did not understand but wanted to know more about. So she ordered a copy of this book, hoping that perhaps it might help explain some of these things.

Miss Borst gave up after two months of teaching, and left for home, so they had an even shorter school term that fall than usual.

Unknown to May and her family at the time, certain "wheels" were set in motion about this time which would eventually lead to great changes in their home and their individual lives.

Mrs. Taylor, a woman who lived on Black Banks Creek three or four miles from the Pettegrews, was a member of the Seventh-day Adventist Church. She wrote a letter to a minister of this denomination who was living in the Black Hills, suggesting that he come to visit the area in which she lived to find out if he thought it a good place to hold a series of meetings. She seemed to think that a number of people might be interested in attending such meetings.

Certain "wheels" were set in motion about this time which would eventually lead to great changes in their home and their individual lives.

The minister to whom she sent the letter, Luther Crothers, may have been in charge of the church work in the Black Hills area at the time and this mission area was perhaps included in the Nebraska Conference of the church organization.

From Hill City, where he lived, Mr. Crothers took the train to Cascade and walked from there the more than twenty miles to the Taylor home. While in the area, he conducted one evening meeting in the little log schoolhouse.

None of May's family attended this meeting, although perhaps May might have done so under different circumstances. The reason they did not attend was because they had been told that the meeting was to be conducted by an Advent preacher.

Selby and his son, Roland, went to hear the Advent preacher, however, for they did not seem to have any such denominational prejudices. Others also attended, and the minister told them that he would return in a few months to hold a series of meetings there.

May's brother and his son told her that they had enjoyed the meeting very much, and that they thought Mr. Crothers was a fine speaker. They were quite interested in what he had preached about, too, so planned to attend the meetings when he returned.

But about this time, May and Alden were making plans for a trip back to eastern Nebraska, so they were too busy to give this matter of religion much consideration. May made some new dresses for herself and little Carrie, who was to go along with them and busied herself getting things in order for when they would be away.

They left in November, and one of the first things they did during their stay in Nebraska was to sell the rest of their old homestead. After visiting with friends and neighbors in the community where they had lived so long, they went on to Fremont to visit Alden's sister Carrie. Here they did some shopping, in preparation for more traveling. One thing Alden bought was a much belated wedding ring for May.

From Fremont they went by train to Denver, Colorado, to visit May's sisters, Kate and Jennie.

While in Denver, Alden and May were entertained quite royally by Kate and her husband, for Kate was the sister who had been taken into the home of well-to-do people after she was orphaned and treated as their own child. She got her diamonds out of the bank vault to wear on one special occasion when they took their guests to the theatre. Little Carrie was just past two years old when she went with her folks on this trip. She could not talk very plainly, but she could sing, for she had been able to carry a tune before she could say the words.

Meanwhile, back at home in South Dakota the children were managing to carry on with the occasional help of their grandparents, aunts, and uncles. Selby did some work on the house for Alden while he was away, putting down a new kitchen floor, because the old one was badly worn. Their grandmother came over and stayed with them some of the time.

Lydia and Ernest had to do the milking, but Lydia had no liking for the job, and still less for having to carry her pail of milk to the house each time after she finished milking a cow. She wanted Ernest to do it for her.

The pail would be too full after milking one cow for her to milk another one in it without first emptying it—or at least part of it. Once, she slipped over to Ernest's pail and poured some from hers into it, and thus she was able to milk another cow before her pail was full. But this caused Ernest's pail to be full before he had finished milking one cow, so he had to empty it, and he wouldn't let Lydia do that anymore.

This just added to Lydia's frustration.

"I'll throw the milk out then," she said threateningly.

She didn't throw it out but carried it to the house and then poured it onto the kitchen floor. It ran all over the floor, of course, and it fell to Suwano, doing the kitchen work, to clean it up. But Ernest did not let this misbehavior on the part of Lydia pass unpunished; he gave her a "good slapping" for it.

Lydia in turn, was not above punishing the younger ones. One morning after breakfast, while she and Suwano were working in the kitchen, Mary and Lou went into the living room to play, and finding some old shoes, they put them on and were walking around in them.

These were shoes much too large for them, and they got the bright idea of kicking them off, each trying to kick them to the ceiling. They were in the middle of the room, kicking them toward the kitchen door, when suddenly the door opened, and who but Lydia came in, just as Lou kicked a shoe off her foot!

The shoe flew over Lydia's shoulder, close by her head, but did not hit her at all. She boxed Lou anyway for the near hit and scolded both girls for playing such a rough game. They realized then that they shouldn't have been kicking the shoes around, but they thought Lydia's punishment was too severe.

The travelers did not return home for Christmas, but they sent gifts for the children: a new saddle for Ernest, new dresses for Lydia and Suwano, and dolls for Mary and Lou.

The children were getting along fine until after Christmas when suddenly Mary got sick, and they did not know what was wrong with her. At first they thought perhaps the can of strawberries they had recently eaten for a treat might be the cause, since that was the only unusual food on their menu, but when Selby came to see them, he immediately diagnosed her condition. Taking one look down Mary's throat, he said, "She has diphtheria."

Chapter 15

Returning Home

As soon as they received a letter from Lydia in which she told them that Mary was ill, Alden and May prepared to return home.

After finding out that it was diphtheria, Selby sent some medicine which had been used for his children when they had diphtheria for Mary to take. Ernest shot some snowbirds, and from these Lydia made soup to tempt Mary's appetite. She was eating this soup when Suwano happened to glance out the window and saw Mr. LaDeau coming. He was bringing their parents from the train.

"Here come the folks," she sang out to the others.

The children were all very glad to see them and gave them a joyous welcome home, but little Carrie scarcely noticed her brother and sisters. From the moment she came in the door and saw that her cat had a family of kittens, she forgot about everything else.

"Oh, my kitties, my kitties!" she exclaimed, running across the room with her arms outstretched toward them.

It was good to be home again. This was May's feeling upon returning after more than a month's absence. She liked to go places and visit people, but it was also good to be at home with all the family and to keep things running smoothly there.

After dinner they all remained seated about the table for quite a while, talking. Alden and May told of their trip, and the children told about what had happened while their parents were away.

"Where's Carrie?" someone asked, suddenly noticing that she was nowhere in sight. They all began looking around and finally found her seated on the floor under the middle of the table around which they had been sitting. She had the wash pan with water in it and a washcloth and was busily occupied with the self-appointed task of washing the front of her new dress. It was a dark colored dress made in the style of the day for little girls, with a wide ruffle around the bottom and a big wide sash around the waist. She had evidently dropped some food on it while eating dinner and wanted to have it cleaned off, so she was doing the job herself.

In the evening Charlie came to visit the returned travelers and to show them a picture of the girl to whom he had become engaged while they were away, Amelia Brattinger. She was a tall girl with very long hair. When standing, with her hair hanging loose, she had only to tip her head a little to one side and her hair would touch the floor.

Like Mary and Lou, Carrie had also received a doll as a Christmas gift from her parents. Mary liked to play with and dress up her dolls, and Carrie liked dolls, too, but Lou did not care much about dolls. She gave one of her dolls to her cousin Perry Barnes.

Mary recovered from her bout with diphtheria, but her hearing was impaired, and this did not seem to improve any with the passing of time. This may have become a greater handicap to her than the rest of the family realized, due to the fact that she did not like to let others know when she did not hear correctly what was said.

Little Carrie Plantz was the next victim of this disease. While taking care of her sister-in-law, Carrie's mother, May noticed that the little girl was allowed to run around in the house barefooted. The floor was cold, for they were having zero weather then, and she caught cold. This complicated her illness and made it much more serious. Little Carrie didn't pull through and the new baby died also, so the two were buried together in a cemetery about half a mile away.

Lydia went to work in Oelrichs again after her parents returned home and was still there when Charlie and Amelia got married. After the wedding, they brought Lydia and the young couple who stood up with them out to the wedding dance that Alden and May gave for them.

May had moved everything out of the living room so it could be used for dancing. All the beds were upstairs, so they made up a bed on boxes under a long table in the kitchen as a place to put the babies to sleep while their parents were dancing. Music for the dance was provided by a neighbor who played the violin with organ accompaniment. Ernest played the organ for part of the dance, but he was not feeling well, so he went to bed early and May took over the chording.

Just before this, while working in Oelrichs, Lydia had joined the Methodist church on probation, and since that denomination did not approve of dancing, some thought that she should not dance at this time. Her father told her that she shouldn't, but she did anyway. So did May and Suwano.

But although they did not know it at the time, this was the last dance they would ever hold in their home.

A series of revival meetings was begun in the little log schoolhouse early in 1893, probably about the time of the wedding. The speaker was the Methodist minister, Mr. Skaggs, from Oelrichs. Ernest, Lydia, and Suwano attended these meetings, also Roland and Pearl Barnes, and of course there were others from outside the family circle who went to the meetings also.

Alden furnished the lights—kerosene lamps they were—for these meetings, and both he and May attended as many of them as they had time for, as did Selby and his wife, Mary, also.

Mary, Lou, and Carrie were left at home, and sometimes Suwano stayed at home with them.

Mr. Skaggs was the sort of preacher who might be talking along smoothly, then suddenly he would yell, or speak loudly, so that most everyone would jump and the babies would cry.

Ernest, Lydia, and Roland began discussing the matter of what church to join, for although they were all seriously considering becoming Methodist, there was that matter of biblical baptism. Lydia still wanted to join the Methodists anyway, but the boys talked some about joining the Baptist church because its doctrines included baptism by immersion rather than by sprinkling. They all knew very well that sprinkling was not biblical.

They argued rather heatedly about this matter for a while, but the final decision was postponed.

"I think we should wait and see what the Advent preacher has to say before we make up our minds about which church to join," Roland remarked one day. It was about time for Mr. Crothers to return and start that series of meetings which he had promised to give.

"Yes, I think so too," Ernest agreed. "I would like to hear what he will say before we decide. Let's wait awhile yet."

"Well, I guess if you boys are going to wait, I will too," Lydia said with some reluctance. She had already decided to become a Methodist, but she was becoming quite fond of her cousin Roland and was not adverse to the prospect of attending another series of meetings with him.

Lydia had once accepted attention from George Brook, Preacher Brook's cowboy son, by allowing him to take her from the Sunday school meeting to her grandparents' home one time, but when her father heard about this, he did not like it one bit, and told her never to go with him again.

However, Alden and May seemed to have no such objections to her going places with Roland, although he was her cousin, for they knew that he was a good boy. The two often went horseback riding together.

When Mr. Skaggs learned of the young folks' interest in baptism, he told them that he would baptize them by immersion if that was what they insisted upon, but he gave them some literature which pretended to show that it was not necessary—that to plunge, dip, pour, or sprinkle were all acceptable modes of baptism. But their decision to hear the Advent preacher's message before joining any church had settled the matter, temporarily at least.

Alden bought about ten head more of cows after he returned from the trip, but the bank where he put the remaining money left from the sale of the homestead in Nebraska went broke in the panic of 1893, so the rest of that money was lost.

Some time afterward, however, they received a small team of horses and a two-seated carriage to compensate in part for the loss of that money. This carriage had a flat top with a fringe around the edge, and it seemed very fine to the youthful members of the family. On the first Sunday after they acquired it, the whole family went out for a ride together in it.

May and her husband had always kept Sunday as a holy day, according to their knowledge and belief about how it should be kept. Alden was a strict Sunday keeper and did nothing on that day which was considered work. To the younger children, especially in the summertime, Sunday seemed like an awfully long day unless someone came to play with them or they went to visit relatives or friends away from home.

> *Just before the close of the Methodist meetings, the Advent minister returned.*

The children were not supposed to play anything that was like work. Mary and Lou were playing together one Sunday when they decided to make a play garden. They got out a hoe and began digging up the ground where they were going to have this garden, but about that time their father came along and saw what they were doing. Alden promptly put a stop to that project, for he felt that it was too much like work and therefore should not be done on Sunday.

Just before the close of the Methodist meetings, the Advent minister returned. Since he had come prepared to hold the promised series of meetings, he stayed until the schoolhouse was available for use.

Alden took his lamps home at the close of the Methodist meetings. He said that he was not going to furnish lights for those Advent meetings, and he had no intention of attending any of the meetings, either. However, he did not forbid his children attending, nor did he ridicule the Adventists as some others were inclined to do.

It is not known how he came to change his mind about the lamps, but they were used for the Advent meetings after all. Perhaps Elder Crothers came and asked to borrow them, and Alden did not have the nerve to say no.

May wanted to attend the meetings from the beginning, but since Alden would not go, she didn't either. Ernest and Lydia were the only members of the family who attended at first, but May's brother, Selby, and some of his family attended. Having been to the meeting Elder Crothers had held in the little log schoolhouse the previous fall, Selby had somehow been impressed in such a way that he felt this man might have a real message of interest to him personally. His wife also attended, and of course Roland, who had encouraged Ernest and Lydia to wait until after hearing the Advent preacher before they decided upon which church they would join.

To help in explaining the prophecies, the minister brought a roll of charts of the sort then used by Adventist preachers. These charts were printed on white muslin and fastened to a pole about the size of a broomstick so they could be rolled up around the pole or hung up on the wall and the pages turned by throwing them up over the pole one at a time.

Suwano, who would soon be thirteen years old, began attending the meetings with her brother and sister. The first evening she went, Lydia and Ernest had already started for the schoolhouse so she borrowed her mother's shawl and went running down the road to catch up with them. They looked back and saw her coming, but it was getting dark, so it was not at first clear to them who or what was coming.

When she caught up with them, they laughingly told her that they thought she was Mr. Evans coming on a mule.

Selby's interest in the Advent message continued, and since an interest in any sort of religion was something new for him, May was anxious that it be encouraged.

"We really ought to go on account of Selby," she said to Alden one day.

"What do you mean?" he asked.

"Well, you know that he has never been at all religious. Perhaps if we would attend these meetings, too, it would encourage him to continue."

"Maybe. But I don't want to get mixed up in anything queer like this Advent religion," was her husband's comment. Then, after a pause, he added, "Yes, there's no doubt about it, some religion would be good for your brother and his family."

"Then let's attend some of the meetings, Alden, shall we?"

Much to May's satisfaction, they, too, began attending the meetings at last, but Alden went with reluctance.

May had not yet had much time to study the book which she had purchased from the colporteur, but she soon found that it contained studies on all the subjects presented by Elder Crothers, as well as some he did not have time to cover in his series of meetings. In it were copies of the same charts which he used to illustrate his sermons on the great lines of prophecy and there, too, the Bible texts were given.

Thus they could look up and read over in question-and-answer form all of the biblical and much of the historical information the minister used in his discourses.

As the great lines of prophecy were explained from the Bible with the help of those charts, a whole new vista of understanding was opened up before the group gathered in the schoolhouse.

History was not an entirely unknown subject to the Pettegrews—they had Gibbons history book—but it was new to them that so much history had been accurately foretold long before in the Scriptures. May had, like most folks, been led to believe that Daniel and Revelation were books which could not be understood, so she had not been interested in their content before. Now all that was soon changed, and she readily accepted the truth as it was presented.

Elder Crothers made it clear that although Daniel had been told to close and seal his book, it was not to remain closed and sealed forever. He quoted the instruction which had been given to Daniel and recorded by him in the fourth verse of the twelfth chapter.

"But thou, O Daniel, shut up the words, and seal the book, even to the time of the end." And again, the prophet was told in the ninth verse, "Go thy way, Daniel, for the words are closed up and sealed till the time of the end."

The prophecy of the four great world empires as revealed in the dream of King Nebuchadnezzar, and Daniel's interpretation of it, were presented, and then the historical fulfillment of this prophecy was explained, including the division of the fourth kingdom into ten parts as represented by the ten toes of the image.

The minister told his listeners that this prophecy was a glimpse of history down through the ages from the time of Daniel to the end of time, for "in the days of these kings shall the God of heaven set up a kingdom, which shall never be destroyed: and the kingdom shall not be left to other people, but it shall break in pieces and consume all these kingdoms, and it shall stand for ever" (Dan. 2:44).

This was followed by a discussion of the signs to herald Christ's return. "And there shall be signs in the sun, and in the moon, and in the stars," was the text, quoted from Luke 21:25.

One of the signs of Christ's coming was particularly interesting to the Pettegrew family. This was the fulfillment of Christ's prophecy in Matthew 24:29 which said, "the stars shall fall from heaven." When Mother Pettegrew heard about this, she told another story of her early life experiences, and thus confirmed the fact among those who heard that there had indeed been a great meteoric shower of shooting stars on November 13, 1833.

"We were traveling by covered wagon at the time," she said. "Our family was camped out for the night, and my bed was made up under the wagon. I was nine years old, and had just gotten all settled in bed there under the wagon, when the stars began falling.

"We all watched them, of course, and thought surely that the end of the world had come. It was just like the Bible description of it in Revelation 6:13 where it says, 'And the stars of heaven fell unto the earth, even as a fig tree casteth her untimely figs, when she is shaken of a mighty wind.' It seemed to me, lying there under the wagon, as if the stars came in between the spokes of the wagon wheels there beside me, and then their light seemed to go out before they touched the ground. It certainly was an awe-inspiring sight to watch that great meteoric shower."

Mother Pettegrew did not attend any of the meetings, but she had become interested in what others told her about them, and the description given so many years before in the Bible of the phenomena she had seen when a girl had increased her interest.

The second coming of Christ was not a new doctrine to the Pettegrew family, but there were a number of things connected with this event which they had not known about before.

May and her family soon began to realize that the last book of the Bible was not, nor had it ever been, a closed or hidden book, impossible to understand. Instead, they found that it is as its author says in the first verse, "the Revelation of Jesus Christ, which God gave unto him, to shew unto his servants things which must shortly come to pass."

The minister pointed out that the apostle Paul said the wicked people living on earth at the time of Christ's second coming will be destroyed "with the brightness of his coming" (2 Thess. 2:8) and "the dead in Christ shall rise" (1 Thess. 4:16). The Pettegrews had believed in the resurrection, and yet, they also had believed that the saved were taken to heaven at death. Elder Crothers took time to straighten out this rather contradictory belief, showing them from the Scriptures that man is mortal, and that it is God "who only hath immortality," as stated in 1 Timothy 6:16.

It was explained that the Christian is not taken to heaven at death, for Peter preached that "David is not ascended into the heavens" in Acts 2:34

but rather, the Bible often speaks of death as a sleep. David wrote of "the sleep of death," in Psalm 13:3, and the words of Christ were quoted in John 11:11 where He said, after being told that Lazarus was dead, "Our friend Lazarus sleepeth; but I go, that I may awake him out of sleep."

Immortality would be bestowed upon the righteous when Christ comes, they were told. "Behold, I shew you a mystery; we shall not all sleep, but we shall all be changed, in a moment, in the twinkling of an eye, at the last trump: for the trumpet shall sound, and the dead shall be raised incorruptible, and we shall be changed. For this corruptible must put on incorruption, and this mortal must put on immortality" (1 Cor. 15:51–53). These texts, and others, were used by the preacher to make this matter better understood.

Through the years, life, death, and many forms of illness had become familiar to May. Since the death of her mother, when she and her little brother stood in awe before the mystery of it all, she had learned many things about life by experience, but until now, death had remained a mystery about which she had learned very little during all those years. She was glad to hear the simple Bible truth of the matter as it was presented by this man of God.

Final events connected with the second coming were made plain by the reading of 1 Thessalonians 4:16–17. "For the Lord himself shall descend from heaven with a shout, with the voice of the archangel, and with the trump of God: and the dead in Christ shall rise first: then we which are alive and remain shall be caught up together with them in the clouds, to meet the Lord in the air: and so shall we ever be with the Lord."

Most people spent their time in or near their homes, working on their own land or perhaps somewhere else nearby, not off in the city at the mill, the factory, the office, or school, so it was possible to make personal contacts more easily then than now. The Adventist minister carried his message into his daily contacts with the people of the community, visiting and conversing with the people on many topics, but always seeking opportunities to further their interest in and knowledge of the Bible and its teachings.

The hospitality of May's home, so often extended to the Methodist ministers was now extended to the Adventist minister as well. One evening soon after his sermon on the state of the dead, Mr. Crothers was invited to supper at the Pettegrew home. While May was in the kitchen getting the meal ready, Ernest came in to talk with her because of something he had been wondering about.

"If the saved don't go to heaven as soon as they pass away, how was it that Moses was with Christ on the mount of transfiguration?" he wanted to know.

"You ask Mr. Crothers about that," May told her son. "He can explain it much better than I can."

Just about then the minister walked into the kitchen where they were, as he had overheard Ernest's question. He explained that sometime after the death and burial of Moses as recorded in Deuteronomy 34:5 and 6, Moses was resurrected and taken to heaven. Evidence of this is in the ninth verse of Jude where reference is made to the devil trying to prevent this from happening. "Michael the archangel, when contending with the devil he disputed about the body of Moses, durst not bring against him a railing accusation, but said, The Lord rebuke thee."

It was noticed that Elder Crothers made it a practice to walk about as May was preparing the meals, during his first few visits in the Pettegrew home, always coming into the kitchen as he had on the occasion of Ernest's question. At first they did not realize just why he did this, but later they knew that he was making a point of being around where he could see what May used in cooking—what foods she cooked in lard or seasoned with pork, so he would know not to eat those foods.

But he found that he had little cause for concern, because May was not much of a hand to use lard. She did most of her seasoning with butter.

During some of his visits to the Pettegrew home, he spent time helping them lathe a room in their house which they were getting ready to plaster.

Scarcely able to carry a tune himself, the minister was able to teach the folks who gathered to hear him quite a number of good Advent hymns. He enjoyed having little Carrie sing for him when he was visiting the family, and taught her a little song, "I dreamed that I was Grandpapa and Grandpapa was me," which she thought was very nice.

One night May's three youngest, Mary, Lou, and Carrie, became unusually fearful at home while the others were away at the meeting. They were afraid someone might come to the house and find them, so they all went into the clothes closet to hide. They thought that no one would find them there and perhaps strangers would not have.

There they fell asleep, so it seemed as if no one was at home when the others returned, but they were soon discovered and sent off to bed.

CHAPTER 16

Accepting Truth

After a biblical description of the new earth as the ultimate and eternal home of the saved, the studies were turned again to the subject of history.

The four beasts in the prophetic vision of Daniel 7 were shown to represent the same four world kingdoms represented in the image of the king's dream, and the ten horns of the fourth beast, like the ten toes, represented the ten kingdoms which developed from the conquest and division of the Roman Empire.

"But the prophecy carries us further down in time than the other one, for here we see the rise of another and different sort of power," the Adventist preacher explained. Then he quoted verse 8: "There came up among them another little horn, before whom there were three of the first horns plucked up by the roots."

That such a power, in the form of the papacy, did develop from pagan Rome and assumed dominion over the nations for a long period of time, often referred to as the Dark Ages, was proven to be historically true.

Perhaps the most interesting part of this prophecy, to May, was the opening scene of the judgment, depicted as following after those Dark Ages. In the last part of the tenth verse Daniel said: "the judgment was set, and the books were opened," and there were a number of other quotations from the Bible, used by Elder Crothers, which mention the judgment, among them the words of Paul in Acts 17:31, where he says that God "hath appointed a day, in the which he will judge the world in righteousness."

The prophetic words of Daniel 8:14, "Unto two thousand and three hundred days; then shall the sanctuary be cleansed," were followed by an explanation of the yearly cleansing ceremony on the Day of Atonement in the Old Testament sanctuary services. This cleansing typified judgment, for that day was a day of judgment for the people of Israel, and their Day of Atonement was a type pointing forward to the final day of God's judgment.

Using the charts depicting this time prophecy and others connected with it, and giving scriptural evidence for its determination, the speaker made clear that those 2,300 days mentioned by Daniel were the 2,300 years from 457 BC to AD 1844.

Portrayal of this investigative judgment as the convening of the supreme court of heaven, and of Christ as our advocate (1 John 2:1), led naturally into the subject of the law which would be used as the standard by which men are judged.

The eternal nature of God's law was emphasized by mentioning that the copy given to Moses in the mount were "tables of stone, written with the finger of God," (Exod. 31:18). It was also pointed out that the underlying principle and reason for keeping the commandments of God is love—love for God and love for man, as represented in the life of Christ in both word and deed.

At the close of his sermon on the law of God, Elder Crothers read from the book of James, chapter 2, verses 10–12: "Whosoever shall keep the whole law, and yet offend in one point, he is guilty of all. For he that said, Do not commit adultery, said also, Do not kill. Now if thou commit no adultery, yet if thou kill, thou art become a transgressor of the law. So speak ye, and so do, as they that shall be judged by the law of liberty."

Among the subjects yet to be presented was one which would stir up more dissension than any other, and yet it would be of the greatest interest to May. This was, of course, the Sabbath, about which she had wondered years before when she had noticed that the fourth commandment read: "the seventh day is the Sabbath of the Lord thy God."

At that first reading she had concluded that Sunday must be the real seventh day, but Alden knew better, and told her so. Now, as the history of the true Bible Sabbath was presented, she learned that her husband had been correct, as far as he knew the truth of the matter.

To begin his studies on the Sabbath question, Elder Crothers said that the seventh-day Sabbath was instituted by God upon this earth at the close of creation week and read Genesis 2:1–3. "Thus the heavens and the earth were finished, and all the host of them. And on the seventh day God ended his work which he had made; and he rested on the seventh day from all his work which he had made. And God blessed the seventh day, and sanctified it: because that in it he had rested from all his work which God created and made."

With this and other texts to back him up, he made it clear that the seventh day of the weekly cycle was set apart for man, that it was the only day ever blessed and sanctified by God, and the only holy day known to man in the beginning. But after Satan succeeded in introducing sin into this world, man was led astray; he drifted away from God and God's plans for him, and thus, it was explained, man was in need of a spiritual revival in his attitude toward the Sabbath as well as in many other things.

May's mind was much impressed with the thought that the Sabbath command was an almost central one in the law of God, and that this set of fundamental principles had been written on stone by the finger of God, showing the eternal nature of each and every one of these Ten Commandments.

Tracing the Sabbath down through the centuries of Bible history, Elder Crothers presented it as unchanged, showed that Christ kept that day while here on earth, and that His followers had continued to keep the seventh day after Christ's return to heaven. Nowhere in the Scriptures could there be found any record of God having authorized a change, nor was any other weekly holy day appointed.

A study of each text in the New Testament which mentioned the first day of the week revealed that there was not even a hint to show that day was to be celebrated in honor of the resurrection.

> *"I'm sending for our minister. I want him to come out here and show us where this Advent preacher is wrong."*

Alden, however, was not easily convinced. He did not like to have his wife accepting all these new doctrines so readily, and he was not satisfied to let them be accepted without some more investigation.

"I want to hear both sides of this Sabbath business," he told May.

"Just what do you mean by that?" she wanted to know.

"I'm sending for our minister. I want him to come out here and show us where this Advent preacher is wrong."

"Oh, so that's it!" she exclaimed. "That is what you have been so quiet about; planning to get Mr. Skaggs to come. Well, we would all like to hear what he will have to say, I think."

So Alden sent word to the Methodist preacher, and Mr. Skaggs sent a reply saying that he could come. Arrangements were made with Elder Crothers for a sort of debate between the two, each of them speaking alternately.

Elder Crothers attended Skaggs' meeting and was asked to offer the prayer. Then the Methodist preached. He claimed that the work of creation was not done in literal days, but seven longer periods of time. He really preached evolution, and told of some folks who lived near Cascade, saying that their place had a stump of a tree which was partly rock when they first moved there, but now it had all turned to rock.

Ernest and Roland saddled up their ponies and rode there one day to find out if this were true. The owner of the place told them that the stump was all rock when they moved onto the place and that there had been no changes in it that he knew anything about since then. But the fact that the stump of a tree had thus changed was evidently supposed to be evidence or proof of the evolutionary theory.

Elder Crothers conducted the next meeting and was easily able to show up Skaggs' theories as false.

Next Skaggs preached that after the resurrection of Christ, Sunday was to be kept. But he did not stay to hear Elder Crothers answer to that; he gave up and left and did not return. Quite some time afterward, the Pettegrew family heard that he had given up preaching altogether.

This debate, brief though it was, served to prove to all who were open-minded enough to accept it, that there had been no biblical change, nor any authorization for such a change, as so many of the Protestant churches seemed to believe.

The question in May's mind at this point, and in the minds of others, too, was obvious. Why did everyone, or most everyone, keep Sunday then? It was the same question she had asked Alden years ago, and he could not give her the answer for, but the Adventist minister had the answer for them.

By this time some of those who had begun attending the meetings at the first had lost interest. Introduction of the Sabbath question was the decisive factor in turning them away and even against the minister and his message. But the Mathwig family continued to attend, and so also did Selby Barnes and his family, the Evans', and the Pettegrews'.

Once again Elder Crothers returned to the prophetic visions of Daniel, pointing out in the seventh chapter, verse 20, that the prophet wished to know more about "that horn that had eyes, and a mouth that spake very great things, whose look was more stout than his fellows," and that Daniel was given more information afterward in verse 25 where he was told that the little horn power would "speak great words against the most High," and "think to change times and laws."

Reference was also made to John's vision of the same power at work, as recorded in Revelation 13, and Paul's words in second Thessalonians the second chapter, verses 3 and 4, warning that the second coming of Christ would not come, "except there come a falling away first, and that man of sin be revealed, the son of perdition; who opposeth and exalteth himself above all that is called God, or that is worshiped; so that he as God sitteth in the temple of God, shewing himself that he is God." Paul added that this "mystery of iniquity doth already work" (verse 7).

Pursuing the thought that this power would "think to change times and laws," the speaker began showing how this was done, as revealed in the history of the early centuries in the Christian era. And herein laid the answer to May's question of such long standing.

Through the gradual uniting of the apostate Roman church with the pagan Roman state, the development of this religio-political power was quite clearly seen in history at this much later time, as it was not so readily recognized while it was being carried out.

May understood that those people and events which were instrumental in establishing Sunday as the man-made day of worship that it is, were none of them alone responsible, but that the power of the evil one was an influence behind them all—that same deceiving power which had led Eve astray.

In her book, *Bible Readings for the Home Circle*, May found quotations from authoritative historical sources, as well as the Bible texts, on this subject of Sabbath versus Sunday. Included was a translation of the pagan Sunday law enacted by the emperor Constantine in AD 321 which is often referred to as the first Sunday law.

This was, of course, not a religious enactment, but a civil law. However, the Roman church was not far behind in completely adopting the "venerable day of the sun" and adapting it to its own purposes. There were quotations from the early church fathers in which they claimed that the church had the authority to change God's law; there was an account of the establishment of the Easter festival, and mention was made of decrees by bishops and church councils meant to transfer the sacredness, duties, and claims of the Sabbath from the seventh day of the week to the first day of the week which they had begun calling "the Lord's Day."

All these May had found in her book of *Bible Readings*, after she learned of them from the meetings.

Also included was a statement from later Catholic Church doctrine in which the claim is made that the church has power to institute holy days because it had successfully changed the Sabbath to Sunday.

All this not only explained very clearly why people keep Sunday, and thus answered her question about that, but it also made it clear to May that the reasons for the observance of Sunday were not good enough for her.

There was much more involved in the apostasy of the early church than its development of Sunday worship, for other pagan rites were also adopted, but it was the change of the day which was of most interest to May and her family. They learned that people had been taught to believe the church had been given the power to make such changes, and to establish whatever rites and ceremonies they chose, and thus was built up in human minds a belief in the authority of the church through its leaders that was never meant to be.

May and her children had little difficulty in accepting the truth as it was unfolded before them. They were prepared, as few others there were, to receive such a message, based as it was upon the Word of God.

But Alden continued to be skeptical and had decided he did not want any of his family to take up with this Sabbath-keeping religion. His next move was to seek information from the Roman Catholic Church itself as to what it might claim in this matter. Thinking that the best way to find out would be to ask, he wrote a letter and sent it to Cardinal Gibbons of Washington, DC asking for the official position of the church on the change.

As Elder Crothers brought his studies on the true Sabbath to a close, he quoted verses 22 and 23 from Isaiah 66: "For as the new heavens and the new earth, which I will make, shall remain before me, saith the LORD, so shall your seed and your name remain. And it shall come to pass, that from one new moon to another, and from one sabbath to another, shall all flesh come to worship before me, saith the LORD."

There were other truths, but dimly understood before, that now became more clear to May. She learned more about spiritualism and now knew that the séances her Uncle Lingner had held were indeed contacts with evil spirits and was but one of many ways in which Satan and his evil angels were perpetuating the deception of mankind begun in the Garden of Eden.

Sunday rapidly lost its former place of importance in the lives of the Pettegrew children and their mother as they came to realize there was no blessing of God upon it, no sacredness involved in that period of time.

Alden stopped attending the meetings before they were brought to an end, and so May again remained at home with him, but the three older children kept right on going, up to and including the very last meeting. At the last one, Elder Crothers asked those to stand who would keep the Sabbath, and Ernest, Lydia, and Suwano were among those who stood.

When they returned home afterward, they told their parents about it.

"There is not going to be any Saturday keeping around here!" Alden told them emphatically.

"You shouldn't talk that way," his wife remonstrated. She had already decided that she would keep the Bible Sabbath, and she knew that he was not as hard-hearted as he sounded. She was still hoping that he would join with her and the children in this decision.

Seventeen gathered for the first Sabbath School ever held in the little log schoolhouse, with Elder Crothers in charge. The Mathwig family was all there, Jim and Coral Smith came, and the Barnes children but not their parents. The three older Pettegrew youths were there in spite of their father's ultimatum.

Roland Barnes was voted in as the superintendent. After the organizing was completed, and the first meeting over, Ernest, Lydia, and Suwano went with their cousins to their home for dinner. As they neared the house, Roland's little brother, Perry, ran ahead of the group.

"Roland is the preacher now," he announced to everyone. The rest of the Pettegrew family had been invited and were already there. Roland was indeed thinking seriously of becoming a minister, planning to be baptized and join the Seventh-day Adventist church at his earliest opportunity.

Along with their cousin, the three Pettegrew youths had also decided to keep the Sabbath, be baptized, and join the church, no matter what their father or anyone else might say.

Some were unwilling to accept the Sabbath truth into their own life experiences, even though they recognized it was the only right way. Such was the case with Mr. Evans, son-in-law of the Mathwigs.

Mr. Evans had been a Sunday school worker, so he was not previously ignorant of religious matters entirely. When the minister stopped by to chat with him, he found the young man readily admitted that he believed the seventh-day Sabbath was right.

"What do you think you should do about it then?" he was asked.

"Keep it," was the reply. But his heart was not really in the words, as subsequent actions proved.

The Mathwig family had been members of the Lutheran church, but now they were planning to become Seventh-day Adventists and were ready to keep their first Sabbath. On Friday, their first preparation day, Mr. Mathwig was working on Mr. Evans' house, plastering the walls, and was so nearly finished with the job that it could have been completed the next day. Mr. Evans insisted that it be finished then. He seemed to think that his father-in-law could just as well wait until the next week to begin his Sabbath-keeping, and he became quite angry when he found that Mr. Mathwig would not.

Selby and Mary Barnes began keeping the Sabbath, but they did not attend the Sabbath School nor accept the message as fully as did their son. Later the influence of Mr. Evans, plus some misconduct of an Adventist they both knew about, seemed to be instrumental in discouraging them more, and they drifted away from the truth which had at first interested Selby so much.

There had been no place in Selby's life for religion of any kind before, and no permanent place was found for it now. He seemed to accept the truth on reason, but reason alone was not enough to make it become a basic part of his way of life.

It is said that devils believe and tremble, and so perhaps with many of us humans. A man may believe yet do little or nothing about putting those beliefs into practice. The end result is that the truth is rejected merely by neglecting to make it a practice which would lead naturally to growth and steadfastness in the Christian way.

As for May, she readily understood that while men may change their laws, and "think to change" the laws of God, they really cannot change God's law at all. He never changes and His laws are everlasting and unchangeable.

Learning which laws are God's and which were only man-made, in the matter of religious practice, had settled what day to keep holy as far as May was concerned. But she did not want to move out ahead of her husband in making the change in church affiliation, because she felt sure that he would join her if she waited for him.

"The seventh-day Sabbath of the Bible commandment seems so right to me now that I understand more about it," she said to Suwano as they worked together in the kitchen one day. "But I was just thinking about how it is with your pa. It is naturally harder for him to take up with something new in religion. He was brought up in a very straightlaced way of thinking about religious matters.

"I remember one time on a Sunday, back in Nebraska, when we were going to visit Aunt Carrie and Uncle Matt. They lived in North Bend then, and on our way, we passed a farm where some people were out working like we would have been working on any other day of the week. They were Seventh-day Adventists—or anyway, I suppose so. Your pa saw them.

"'There ought to be a law to keep them from working on Sunday,' he said to me. He seemed to be truly sincere in his belief that forcing people to observe Sunday would be a good thing and the way religion should be practiced."

As her mother was talking, Suwano was thinking back, too, remembering her father's attitude about what the children should or should not do on the first day of the week.

"One time when Cousin Ethel was out to our place on Sunday," she began, "we girls started playing a game running after each other, Lydia, Ethel, and I. We went running through the front room where Pa was sitting, and he put a stop to that right off. He said to Lydia and me 'You sit down in a chair, each of you, and don't get up until I tell you that you can.'

"So we sat down, and had to stay there, and be quiet, too, for some time. We didn't even talk."

"Yes, he has been particular about you children keeping Sunday, as well as in keeping it himself, as he thought it should be kept."

"Do you remember the Sunday when Ernest and Lydia took a wooden tub across the creek?" Suwano asked her mother with a smile.

"Yes, I certainly do. They took a rope that was long enough to reach across the creek. Lydia held one end of the rope and Ernest tied the other to the tub on the opposite side of the creek. Then he got into the tub and Lydia was to pull him across. But the tub didn't make a very good boat. It upset and Ernest had to come to the house and put on dry clothes."

"Then you scolded him," Suwano added. "You told him, 'That is what you get for doing a stunt like that on Sunday!'"

"We have always tried to do what we thought was right," her mother observed.

Alden soon had an answer to the letter he had sent to Washington. The Cardinal wrote him that the Catholic Church had indeed made the change in the day of worship and made claim that the church had the power to do this. He also sent Alden a subscription to the *Catholic Mirror*.

Elder Crothers asked those to stand who would keep the Sabbath, and Ernest, Lydia, and Suwano were among those who stood.

After receiving this personally satisfactory proof that the Catholic church had thus fulfilled the prophecy of Daniel's vision, Alden permitted Elder Crothers to come and give him a study on the Sabbath. The chart was put up in the home and the material on the history and change of the day presented.

Finally he told the minister that he would keep the Sabbath, but he would not, he said with a tone of finality in his voice, join the church. Some of his relatives were bitterly opposed to the idea of any of the family joining this "queer" church, so it was largely because of family opposition that Alden refused to become a member, although he accepted the message.

Like many others, the Pettegrews were a rather closely knit family. To some of them the form and acceptability of one's religious connections were very important, and they were prejudiced against anything which seemed to be considered odd by the general public. Having been unable to ignore the new religion altogether, Alden had sought to have it disproved because he felt it was entirely unacceptable, and he did not want to have some of his family belonging to a church so different from the popular ones.

Failing in this, but having it proved to be correct instead, he was too honest to persist in his objections. He knew it was the truth, and he also admitted that it was, but to placate his family he would not make public his beliefs at this time.

Of his family, it was Alden's sister, Carrie, who was the most prejudiced. After she heard of the interest some of her family had taken in this queer religion, she had come to show them the error of their thinking, and her words had their intended effect upon her mother. Not that Mother Pettegrew disbelieved the message, but because of Carrie's effort, she seemed to feel it would be too difficult for her to ever change her religious affiliations.

May became a member of the Seventh-day Adventist church on profession of faith, as she had already been baptized by immersion. The wedding ring so recently acquired she gave to the gospel cause at this time.

The young folks kept the little Sabbath School going in the log schoolhouse, and occasionally a minister of the church would come and give a sermon afterward. Then some others, including Alden and May would go, and the younger children were taken along.

While the change in their day of worship was the most outstanding change which came into their lives, there was also a change in their diet. After they quit using pork, it was noticed that Suwano's health was much improved. Soon afterward, Alden got rid of his hogs.

Camp meeting time, late in the summer of 1893, found Roland Barnes, Ernest, Lydia, and Suwano Pettegrew and Alden's sister, Lou, on their way to Crawford, Nebraska, in a covered wagon to attend the meetings. They found the campground just across a branch of the White River, to the west of the town.

They had no place to stay except in the wagon, but the Crothers family took the girls in with them to sleep in their tent, so Roland and Ernest had the wagon to themselves.

The Mathwig family also attended this camp meeting. Mr. and Mrs. Mathwig, three of their children, Ernest, Fred, and Herman, Roland Barnes, and the Pettegrew youths, Ernest, Lydia, and Suwano, all were baptized at the camp meeting in the White River and became members of the Seventh-day Adventist church.

Although Alden did not join the church organization, it was not at all a divided home, for he began living the truth along with the members of his immediate family.

To thus have her dearest ones joined with her in the blessed hope meant a great deal to May. Looking back over the years, she began thinking that they might have missed the chance to hear these truths had they remained in Nebraska, and to her it was worth all it had cost them to give up the good home there and come to the Dakota plains to start over again. There in Nebraska they might have been too busy—become so occupied and established with social, community, and church affairs that perhaps none of them would have cared to attend a series of meetings like these even if the opportunity had come.

> **She began thinking that it was worth all it had cost them to give up the good home and come to the Dakota plains to start over again.**

Conclusion

Many years were still ahead for Melissa May; years filled with change, tragedy, joy, service, and faith. But that would be another story. However, a glimpse into the near future reveals the death of Father Pettegrew in 1895, the birth of another daughter, Lelia Sylvanus, in 1897, and finally, in 1901, the baptism of Alden. He became a member of the Seventh-day Adventist church at that time, along with Mary and Lou.

During the 1890s, the church organization was still rather loosely held together, especially at the "grass roots," in such outlying areas as that of this story. Evidently, workers from eastern Nebraska had been sent into the Panhandle to the west, over into Wyoming, and up into the Black Hills. This was, as far as is known, continued until the organizing of the Wyoming Mission in 1904.

Although Melissa May had not been able to get much formal education, it was enough to help keep her always a learner. Her search for knowledge did not cease when she found the truth and began to walk more fully in the light of God's Word, but she kept an open mind without ever losing sight of eternal values.

Conformity to the immediate world about us, and aggressiveness in the pursuance of material things are all too prevalent and important among those of us today who profess Christianity. How we need to get back to the true fundamental principles and use them as she did on which to build for eternity, each in our own way and to the best of our abilities.

Had she lived in our Atomic Age, Melissa May would surely have been able to take it in stride, having early learned adaptability, for she adjusted to numerous changes and to all sorts of people and circumstances—some of them kind and some not so kind. She learned to use to the best of her ability those talents entrusted to her, and as she met the problems of life, her capabilities grew and developed, her faith increased, and she was constantly finding new ways in which she could be of service to others.

Home

Out on the wild waste of prairie
      A house all alone you will find.
The snow rushes madly around it
      Forced on by the fierce bitter wind.

Within its kind walls there is shelter
      For a family happy and gay.
The father and mother and daughters
      Each busy with work or with play.

The parents sit by the warm fireside
      With a smile that includes every one;
Suwano is mending her saddle;
      Carrie's shoe is just about done.

Busy with art sits fair Mary,
      Wielding her brush with such skill
That wondrous creations of flowers
      Appear on the white page at will.

With needle and thread sits another
      Her pillow will soon be complete;
But Lou says her pillow is never
      For anyone's head or their feet.

Lela, the youngest among them,
      Is busier than all the rest;
And thus time passes so swiftly
      Night soon overshadows the nest.

Each day brings its pleasures or sorrows;
      Both are welcomed with honest goodwill.
So day unto day passes onward,
      All duties they ably fulfill.

(Gertrude Spiker, 1905)

Melissa May and Alden in young adulthood; this is thought to be the photo mentioned in chapter 7.

Melissa May at age 93 in June, 1947, seated in a wheelchair after breaking her hip.

Left to right: Lydia, Suwano, Mary, Lou, and Lela, date unknown

TEACH Services, Inc.
PUBLISHING

We invite you to view the complete
selection of titles we publish at:
www.TEACHServices.com

We encourage you to write us
with your thoughts about this,
or any other book we publish at:
info@TEACHServices.com

TEACH Services' titles may be purchased in
bulk quantities for educational, fund-raising,
business, or promotional use.
bulksales@TEACHServices.com

Finally, if you are interested in seeing
your own book in print, please contact us at:
publishing@TEACHServices.com

We are happy to review your manuscript at no charge.

www.ingramcontent.com/pod-product-compliance
Lightning Source LLC
Chambersburg PA
CBHW070555160426
43199CB00014B/2509